DOES
GOD
EXIST?

DOES
GOD
EXIST?

BOBBY CONWAY

HARVEST HOUSE PUBLISHERS
EUGENE, OREGON

This book is dedicated to my lifelong friend Jonathan Ross,
for entertaining a thousand questions and more.
Thank you for believing in me and helping me live the inquisitive life.

Cover by Dual Identity, Inc.

Published in association with William K. Jensen Literary Agency, 119 Bampton Court, Eugene, Oregon 97404.

DOES GOD EXIST?

Copyright © 2016 Bobby Conway
Published by Harvest House Publishers
Eugene, Oregon 97402
www.harvesthousepublishers.com

ISBN 978-0-7369-6262-9 (pbk.)
ISBN 978-0-7369-6263-6 (eBook)

Printed in the United States of America

16 17 18 19 20 21 22 23 24 / VP-JC / 10 9 8 7 6 5 4 3 2 1

CONTENTS

Foreword

What book would you recommend for my son? I raised him as a Christian, but he's not a believer any more. Every time we talk, he bombards me with questions. I need better answers. Sometimes I'm not even sure where to begin."

Emails like this one (from the father of a 19-year-old university student) appear regularly in my inbox. I'm not sure which is more discouraging: the growing number of young Christians who are walking away from the Church, or the regular despair I hear from parents who seem ill-equipped to answer their kid's questions. As a youth pastor, I saw the problem with my own eyes. We live in a culture that is less accepting of Christianity than ever before. It's an *aggressive* culture driven by media, technology, and information. If young Christians are to survive in this setting, we, as the Church, need to be ready "to make a defense to everyone who asks [us] to give an account for the hope that is in [us]" (1 Peter 3:15), by leveraging the media, technology, and information age in which we live.

No one is doing this better than the One-Minute Apologist, Bobby Conway. When I first discovered one of Bobby's videos and watched him make the case for Christianity in a brief, powerful, online presentation, I thought, "Dang, why didn't I think of that?" Bobby has been interviewing "the world's leading apologists to provide credible answers to curious questions" for several years now, and he's addressed hundreds of questions, challenges, and objections to the existence of God. He's been sitting across the microphone from the best Christian Case Makers in the land; he's heard every objection and considered every reasonable response.

More importantly, he's learned how to engage the culture.

Bobby's video ministry is a "gateway" ministry, introducing believers and skeptics to experts in the field while presenting brief responses to the objections offered by the culture. These videos have been viewed by thousands of people who are looking for an answer, a starting point, or a word of encouragement. Bobby's visual, targeted, culturally relevant approach has helped many people navigate their doubts and strengthen their faith.

Now Bobby has taken what he's learned sitting alongside the best apologists and crafted another effective resource for those who have questions about God. Like his video ministry, *Does God Exist?* is concise, targeted, and culturally relevant. If you've got a question about God, I bet there's an answer in this book. *Does God Exist?* reflects the diversity of Bobby's One-Minute Apologist videos. You'll find responses to important metaphysical questions, refined theological issues, and timely moral concerns. Bobby will help you address the culture effectively even as you answer your own doubts and concerns. This is a book you'll return to often.

I know the temptation with books like these, however. You will definitely want to give this book to your kids, family members, or friends who have questions about Christianity. It's perfect for the father who emailed me about his son. But let me caution you: *Does God Exist?* is more than a book you can *give away*. It's a book *you* need to read and master. This is an incredibly accessible resource; you can easily train yourself to make the case for Christianity by reading each chapter and watching the associated videos. So take the time to examine its contents, think about what you've learned, consider the questions at the end of each chapter, and research the expert case makers Bobby has introduced. *Does God Exist?* will show you where to begin and help you respond with better answers.

J. Warner Wallace, Cold-Case Detective and Author of
Cold-Case Christianity and *God's Crime Scene*

Introduction

Are you the inquisitive type? And do you find yourself a little on the curious side? Were you the child always raising your hand in class? If so, that's nothing to be ashamed of. Asking questions is part of the learning process. *Great learners ask great questions.* And there is no such thing as a dumb question—*if* you're genuinely seeking to learn. Regrettably, many people stunt their learning simply because they're too embarrassed to ask questions. That's unfortunate.

But think about it. The only person who doesn't *need* to ask questions is God. That's because He knows everything. God doesn't need to raise His hand. He doesn't use Google. And He certainly hasn't enrolled in a PhD program. He's all-knowing. Theologians refer to this as God's *omniscience*. Must be nice, huh?

So we think. But would you want to know everything?

The good.

The bad.

And the ugly?

I don't think so. Maybe the good, but certainly not all the ugly. Lord knows there's enough going on in the world that we don't need stuck in our heads. We can be thankful for some good

9

old-fashioned ignorance—for God's shrouded grace. It even seems that God wanted Adam and Eve to remain in the dark about the ugly (see Genesis 2:15-17).

Curiosity taken to its extreme can be dangerous. There are some things that we must be content not knowing—things that reach beyond the finite. That should be freeing. But fortunately, there's a lot that we can know. And should know. While we can't discover the answers to all our questions, we can find the answers to some of them.

I'm thankful for that.

For many years I've been passionate about tracking down the answers not only to other people's questions but also to my own. I have the privilege of hosting an internationally recognized program called *The One-Minute Apologist* where our motto is "providing credible answers to curious questions." And that's what I hope to do in this book. I'm seeking to do in written form what I already do through my weekly videos. My aim is to provide short answers to sincere questions. Also, to help maximize your curiosity quest, I've included at the end of each chapter a thought to ponder, a memory verse, a question to consider, and a corresponding video from my *One-Minute Apologist* YouTube program.

It's my hope that this little book will get you thinking more about God and the Bible.

Before getting started, let me make an important qualification. The answers in this book are by no means exhaustive. Far from it. Rather, they're pithy and to the point.

In the end, this is simply a Q&A book about God and the Bible. With that in mind, I invite you to use this book in your quiet times, during your family devotions, as a gift for new believers or those interested in what Christians believe, or even with your friends as you journey toward a more thoughtful Christianity.

Does God Exist?

*On our total evidence theism is
more probable than not.*

RICHARD SWINBURNE

Some questions carry more weight than others. Such is the case with the question, "Does God exist?" People will often contend that God does exist (theism), or He *may* exist (agnosticism), or He doesn't exist (atheism). If it can be shown that He does exist, the latter two options are irrelevant.

Think about it. God can't exist and not exist, right? He either is or He isn't. Even the agnostic would concede that God either exists or He doesn't. The agnostic doesn't refute that point. Rather the agnostic pleads the fifth when it comes to knowing how to settle the answer to the question of God's existence. What can we say by means of support for theism?

First, the Bible presupposes God's existence. It's as if the Scriptures knew God's existence would be brought into question. Therefore, from the very first verse of the Bible the rumor is dispelled as it opens with the phrase, "In the beginning, *God*" (Genesis 1:1).

Second, to deny God's existence is to deny the obvious. When we fast-forward to the New Testament we learn that God's not hiding out. No. He's not playing hide-and-seek. Rather, He has made Himself known. In Romans 1:19-20 we read, "What can be known about God is *plain* to them, because God has *shown* it to them. For his invisible attributes, namely, his eternal power and divine nature, have been *clearly perceived*, ever since the creation of the world, in the things that have been made. So *they are without excuse*." Paul is stressing that the evidence for God's existence is clear. It's as if he's saying, "No one can play curious in the midst of the obvious." Creation shouts, "We're not here by accident!" Even atheists will concede, "Yes, it looks as if the universe is designed, but it's not." What are they doing? Rejecting the obvious. Rejecting God's existence.

Third, it's foolish to deny God's existence. So confident is David in the obviousness of God's existence that he quips, "The fool says in his heart, 'There is no God'" (Psalm 14:1). And yet, note the irony. Today, the mantra has been flipped. Ours is a culture that says, "The fool says in his heart, 'There is a God.'" Well, is there? And if He does exist, are there any hints out there? Indeed. This leads to our final point.

Fourth, to deny God's existence is to reject the evidence. For starters, the universe had a beginning. And the evidence for such a claim is robust. With Einstein's universally embraced theory of general relativity and its claim that space, time, and matter all had a starting point, the argument for a beginning is powerfully complementary to scientific theories. Subsequent to Einstein's discovery, the Hubble Space Telescope enabled us to see that the universe we live in is expanding. If the expansion process could be reversed, the universe would be brought back to a beginning point. Eureka.

So what does all this mean? It means the universe and everything in it had a cause, including you and including me. Something can't come from nothing, right? But you say, "According to your logic, wouldn't God need a cause too?" Nope. And that's because God didn't *begin* to exist. He is self-existent. He's a necessary being, the uncreated Creator of all things. He's in a league of His own. He is...the great I am. The self-existent One.

Next, consider the intricate design all around us. So much so that, as I said, even the skeptics concede that the universe looks like someone's been tinkering with it. Or better yet, has tailored it. Then there's DNA, a code so information-rich that it's hard to imagine how such intelligence could surface from non-intelligence.

Finally, consider our innate sense of right and wrong. Where does that come from? As humans, we come into this world with God's moral code branded on us. According to Scripture, God's moral law has been inscribed on each of our hearts (Romans 2:14-15). A moral law requires a moral lawgiver, and that giver is God. Sure, some contend that there's no such thing as wrong. But wrong him and he will be the first to say, "Hey, what's up with that? That wasn't right!"

While some maintain that God doesn't exist, they cannot with integrity claim that to believe in God is a mere fantasy and there is no warrant for such belief. The warrant is everywhere.

■ Thought to Ponder

Isn't it ironic that so many people who pride themselves on being mindful believe that the universe is the product of mindlessness?

■ Memory Verse

The fool says in his heart, "There is no God" (Psalm 14:1).

■ Question to Consider

With all of this evidence at believers' disposal, why do atheists still insist that believers are so naïve and ignorant for their so-called illusory belief in God?

■ One-Minute Apologist Video

Ken Boa, "Does God Exist?"
www.youtube.com/watch?v=x2iZHCBMN1Y

Who Made God?

> *To ask, "Who made God?" commits a category*
> *fallacy: It assumes that God is a contingent*
> *(dependent), caused entity. God by definition*
> *is uncaused and eternally existent.*
>
> Paul Copan

Asking the question, "Who made God?" is like asking, "How did Beethoven's Moonlight Sonata taste?" It just doesn't fit. The question is a classic category mistake. Why? Because God wasn't made and the Moonlight Sonata can't be tasted! Adding to this blunder, the famed atheist Bertrand Russell notoriously said, "If everything must have a cause, then God must have a cause." But it's not true that everything must have a cause. Only that which *begins* to exist must have a cause. And herein God is perched up in a category of His own.

God is the uncreated Creator. He is the beginning-less Beginner. He is the uncaused Cause of all that exists. Think about it. Everything that had a beginning had a Beginner. Every product has a Producer. And every initiative must have an Initiator. If there is an origin there must be an Originator. And since there is a genesis there is a Generator. That generator is God.

Exclaimed from verse one of the Bible the Scriptures announce, "In the beginning, God created the heavens and the earth" (Genesis 1:1). Far from being made, God is the Maker of all things. He is the Cause of all first causes. He is the Producer of all that was originally produced. He's the original Originator. And the Genesis of all that's been generated!

Do you remember what God said to Moses when He appeared to him in the burning bush to appoint him to confront Pharaoh?

> Moses said to God, "If I come to the people of Israel and say to them, 'The God of your fathers has sent me to you,' and they ask me, 'What is his name?' what shall I say to them?" God said to Moses, "I AM WHO I AM." And he said, "Say this to the people of Israel, 'I AM has sent me to you'" (Exodus 3:13-14).

What was God saying to Moses? He was revealing Himself to Moses as the *self-existent* one. As the one who wasn't made! God was saying, "Moses, go tell them that the One who never began to exist sent you. The unmade One."

Unlike us, God is a necessary being, an independent being. And each of us, unlike God, are contingent beings, therefore, dependent. The universe is also contingent. God spoke it into existence. This means all things that began to exist are dependent on God for existence.

It turns out there is a problem with the question "Who made God?" The word *made* can't be said of God. For God is the unmade Maker.

■ Thought to Ponder

It's been said, "It's a whole lot easier to believe that Something took nothing and made something than it is to believe that nothing took nothing and made something."

■ Memory Verse

Before the mountains were brought forth, or ever you had formed the earth and the world, from everlasting to everlasting you are God (Psalm 90:2).

■ Question to Consider

Why are so many people content to believe that everything came from nothing?

■ One-Minute Apologist Video

Frank Turek, "Who Created God?"
https://www.youtube.com/watch?v=1yY9a2SwNx4

Did God Create the World to Boost His Own Glory?

Let me be clear that of course the Bible says it is our obligation to love, praise, and worship God, but this is a very different matter from the suggestion that God worships himself, is deeply worried about whether he has enough glory or not, and his deepest motivation for doing anything on earth is so that he can up his own glory quotient, or magnify and praise himself.

BEN WITHERINGTON

Some people have a hard time stomaching the idea of a relationship with the Christian God because they think He created the world for a personal glory boost. Sort of like creating a world destined for redemption in order to become your own superhero.

How can we respond to such a view?

First, God didn't create the world with a desire for us to rebel against Him. Rather, the world was created in perfection and declared "good" by God (see Genesis 1:31).

Second, it wasn't God's desire for evil to enter into the world. In fact, He even warned Adam to avoid the tree of knowledge of good and evil (Genesis 2:16-17).

Third, God didn't create the universe and all of humanity

because there was something lacking within Him. He has no defi-
ciency. No need. We weren't created for His emotional fulfillment.
The thought in itself is absurd, if not laughable. Nor does God have
some deep-rooted insecurity issue whereby He created us so that
we could remind Him of how great He is. He's well aware. And
not arrogantly so, but obviously so!

Fourth, neither did God create us because He suffered from
the horrors of loneliness. God is triune. He has eternally existed
in what Alvin Plantinga, the eminent philosopher, refers to as the
"Charmed circle of the Trinity."* God is a communal God. One
God eternally existing in triune community!

So why did God create us? Not for lack. Rather God created
us to share Himself with us. Far from being a selfish megaloma-
niac, God is a selfless, giving, omnibenevolent God. His greatest
act of benevolent love was witnessed at Calvary in the Person of
Jesus Christ as He sought to rescue us from the consequences of
this macabre, marked world. It was there at Golgotha that Christ
shared in our suffering to atone for our sins. And it wasn't out of
His need. It was out of ours.

■ Thought to Ponder

God didn't create us to boost His own glory. That would imply
He was in need of us. Rather, He created us to share in His glory
and to experience His creation and ultimately to know Him as
our Creator.

---

* Alvin Plantinga, *Knowledge and Christian Belief* (Grand Rapids, MI: Eerdmans, 2015), 123.

■ **Memory Verse**

The God who made the world and everything in it, being Lord of heaven and earth, does not live in temples made by man, nor is he served by human hands, as though he needed anything, since he himself gives to all mankind life and breath and everything (Acts 17:24-25).

■ **Question to Consider**

What would that say about God if He created the world to boost His own glory?

■ **One-Minute Apologist Video**

Bobby Conway, "Did God Create the World to Boost His Own Glory?"

https://www.youtube.com/watch?v=lMUqwjeEbrc

God, Who Are You?

> *What comes into our minds when we think about*
> *God is the most important thing about us.*
>
> A.W. TOZER

At the ripe old age of five, the great thirteenth-century philosopher and theologian Thomas Aquinas asked his teacher, "What is God?" His teacher was stumped. As a result, Thomas became a theologian to find out for himself. Regarding God's essence, he didn't think we could answer that question. But he did believe we could know that God exists. Thanks to Aquinas, we are privy to so much great work in the area of natural theology.

As Christians, we believe that God has made Himself known through both **natural and special revelation**. *Natural revelation* refers to knowledge of God that can be obtained through philosophy, human reason, and observation of nature. Arguments from nature such as the cosmological argument, the fine-tuning argument, or even the moral argument (see chapter 1) help us to learn *some* things about the nature of God, even demonstrating that life is not an accident. By studying the philosophical and scientific arguments for God's existence we can see that God is a necessary, uncaused, timeless, spaceless, and immaterial creator God.

We can be thankful that those arguments provide a compelling case for God's existence, but these are also arguments that other theists like Jews and Muslims can utilize. Fortunately, God has made Himself even clearer through *special revelation*—that is, through Scripture and through the person of Jesus Christ. And we need special revelation to answer the question before us.

Namely, *Who is God?*

As we should expect, Scripture confirms through special revelation what we've already learned about God through natural theology. But special revelation seasons things up a bit by supplying more flavorful detail about God. Here's a mere sampling of what we learn about God.

- God is omnipresent (Psalm 139:7-12; Jeremiah 23:24)

- God is omniscient (Psalm 147:4-5)

- God is omnipotent (Jeremiah 32:17; Psalm 135:6)

- God is Spirit (John 4:24)

- God is in a league of His own (Isaiah 46:9)

- God is immortal and invisible (1 Timothy 1:17)

- God is the Creator (Genesis 1:1; Colossians 1:16)

- God is unchanging (Malachi 3:6)

- God is sovereign (Psalm 115:3)

- God is One, yet He exists in three persons (Matthew 3:16-17; 28:19; 2 Corinthians 13:14)

- God is loving (John 3:16; 1 John 4:8)

- God is gracious and merciful (Jonah 4:2; Deuteronomy 4:31)

- God is righteous (Psalm 11:7)

- God is holy (Leviticus 19:2; 1 Peter 1:16)

- God is just (Deuteronomy 32:4; Isaiah 30:18)

- God is forgiving (1 John 1:9)
- God is compassionate (James 5:11)

This is just a snapshot of who God is. I'm guessing you get the picture. We serve a pretty special God—a God who deserves our highest devotion, our deepest love, and our fullest gratitude.

Thought to Ponder
God is a God who is to be more than defined. He's to be loved.

Memory Verse
Behold, God is great, and we know him not; the number of his years is unsearchable (Job 36:26).

Question to Consider
If you had to best summarize who God is based on the biblical data we have at our disposal, what would you say?

One-Minute Apologist Video
Bobby Conway, "Who Is God?"
https://www.youtube.com/watch?v=Djn_etbdw7g

Will There Be Sex in Heaven?

I think our present outlook might be like that of a small boy who, on being told that the sexual act was the highest bodily pleasure should immediately ask whether you ate chocolates at the same time. On receiving the answer "No," he might regard absence of chocolates as the chief characteristic of sexuality. In vain would you tell him that the reason why lovers in their carnal raptures don't bother about chocolates is that they have something better to think of. The boy knows chocolate: he does not know the positive thing that excludes it. We are in the same position. We know the sexual life; we do not know, except in glimpses, the other thing which, in Heaven, will leave no room for it.

C.S. LEWIS

Will there be sex in heaven? The short answer is no. But I've got some explaining to do, right? Here are a few reasons why there won't be sex in heaven.

First of all, sex has a setting, a turf or a milieu. Call it a terrain. And the stomping ground where sex takes place is in the context of marriage here on earth until death do us part. Unlike Muslims and Mormons who believe that there will be sex in the afterlife, the Christian challenges that conclusion on biblical grounds. On one occasion, while addressing the Sadducees, Jesus said, "In the resurrection they neither marry nor are given in marriage, but are like angels in heaven" (Matthew 22:30).

Secondly, there won't be a need for sex in heaven. Imagine that. Sex on earth is for the two-fold purpose of procreation (Genesis 1:28) and mutual pleasure (Proverbs 5:15-19), and this double feature is reserved only for you and your spouse (Proverbs 5:20). In fact, adultery is seriously forbidden (Exodus 20:14; 1 Corinthians 6:9). Now fast-forward to heaven. Why won't there be sex?

As it relates to procreation there won't be any need to further populate heaven with more children. Regarding sexual pleasure, all of our deepest desires, needs, longings, and pleasures will be fully met by God. Trust me. You won't feel like you're missing out. In heaven, while our unique gender distinctions of male and female will be preserved, there will only be one bride—the Church. And there will only be one Groom in heaven—Christ. It'll be a perfect match. Call it a match made in heaven. Quite literally!

▧ Thought to Ponder
Heaven will be a lust-free paradise marked by a perfect love—a godly love.

▧ Memory Verse
For in the resurrection they neither marry nor are given in marriage, but are like angels in heaven (Matthew 22:30).

▧ Question to Consider
Why do you think it's so hard to imagine a world without sexual intimacy?

▧ One-Minute Apologist Video
Bobby Conway, "Will There Be Sex in Heaven?"
https://www.youtube.com/watch?v=zuWoKhtU7I0

What's the Big Deal About Premarital Sex?

I have had plenty of people say, "Well, what's wrong with sex outside of marriage?" The answer is the Bible says God invented sex as a way to say to somebody else that I belong completely and exclusively to you. So if you use sex to say something else you really destroy the ability of sex to work because sex is a covenant renewal ceremony.

TIMOTHY KELLER

Why in the world would God want a couple to wait until they're married before having sex? Could He possibly have good reasons—or is He simply out of touch? Isn't God a bit Victorian in His sexual approach? Isn't it time we freshen Him up a bit and help Him be a little more culturally relevant?

Well, not so fast. Let's think about this for a moment. What could God's agenda possibly be for having us wait until we're married to have sex?

First, God desires our marital relationships to have maximum trust. He's not trying to spoil the fun, nor is He seeking to be a party pooper. He knows how important the trust factor is to marriage. By waiting, a couple is able to establish a foundation of trust. Consider this: If you're dating a person who is willing to have sex with you, then you're dating a person who is willing to sleep with an unmarried person. What makes you think when you get married your spouse still won't be willing to have a little sex outside of marriage?

My wife and I are on the national speaking team for Family-Life. At one of the Weekend to Remember events one of our speakers was approached by a lady who said, "Before my husband and I were married we would have sex. He'd often say, 'I can't wait—I can't wait.' So we had sex. But now that we are married, he travels a lot and I wonder what will happen if he can't wait and I'm not there." See how her trust was fractured as a result of premarital sex? When a couple waits to have sex until they're married, they're revealing to each other that they have the self-control that's necessary to handle their sexual passions. And this creates trust—*the* necessary ingredient to a healthy marriage.

Second, there would be no such thing as STDs if we just followed God's plan. God obviously had some wisdom regarding sex outside of marriage. Our way of doing things has resulted in countless deaths through AIDS, and millions of people have suffered the consequences of sexually transmitted diseases. Want to avoid contracting AIDS and all other forms of STDs? Have sex God's way—in the context of marriage.

Third, premarital sex builds the relationship in **reverse** order. We are to date the soul and then sex becomes the celebration of our oneness through the marital covenant. We date the soul and marry the body *and* soul. Premarital sex inserts a false set of emotions into the relationship. And as a result, sexually active couples often think they're closer to each other than they really are. That's because sex is powerful. This creates a false sense of compatibility when in reality the couple may be at odds relationally. By dating the soul you can first establish your friendship and evaluate whether you're compatible for one another. Don't put the cart before the horse. I've met many people who have regretted not waiting, but I've never met one couple that regretted waiting.

The wait is worth it.

Now that's worth pondering!

As we wrap up this question, let me say a word to those who have already had sex outside of marriage—to those perhaps living with regret. I can relate. I was very promiscuous before I gave my life to Christ and even for a season after becoming a believer. Fortunately, my wife and I were able to date for nearly two years before we got married and we did wait. I'm so thankful we did. It really created a deep sense of trust for each other, especially for Heather considering my promiscuous past. She saw that I was able to wait—for her. Needless to say, if you've got regrets, know that God is a forgiving God (1 John 1:9). And if you're in a sexual relationship, make a decision together to wait. You won't be sorry. I promise.

▣ Thought to Ponder

If you want maximum trust in your marriage it'll mean submitting your lusts to God and waiting to act out on your sexual passion until the right time—until you say, "I do."

▣ Memory Verse

A man without self-control is like a city broken into and left without walls (Proverbs 25:28).

▣ Question to Consider

What are the lies our culture tells us about why we should have sex before marriage?

■ One-Minute Apologist Video

Bobby Conway, "What's the Big Deal About Having Premarital Sex?"

https://www.youtube.com/watch?v=5FZPPEZa6aM

What's Wrong With Pornography?

> *Pornography takes human sexuality*
> *out of its natural context—intimacy*
> *between two human beings—and makes*
> *it a product to be bought and sold.*
>
> WILLIAM M. STRUTHERS

A few years back I was talking to an old friend on the phone. At one point during the conversation I was discussing the importance of avoiding pornography. He chimed in and said, "What's wrong with porn, man? I love porn." Well, he's not alone. So do millions of other people. That's why it's a multi-billion dollar industry. But what is it about pornography that we should pay serious attention to? And be cautious of?

First, porn objectifies women. Or all people for that matter. The options for porn material are limitless. There's homosexual porn, child porn, and of course adult female porn. We objectify people when we use them for our own self-centered purposes. That's what porn does. It uses people. It treats them like objects. It objectifies them! Porn is using an image of a human being made in the image of God to gratify one's lustful desires. And that's not good.

Second, porn destroys our brain. Seriously. It causes brain damage. Let me explain. With the advancement of neuroscience we now know that our willpower is a function of the prefrontal lobe of the brain. Consistent use of pornography actually reshapes this critical part of the brain, thus weakening one's moral fortitude. The will is sapped of strength through continuous porn play. It's often referred to as *hypofrontality*. This breakdown of the frontal lobe of the brain especially affects addicts. Their addictive desires heighten while their determination to resist is weakened and buckles under sexual pressure. Next time you find yourself tempted to look at pornography just remind yourself that porn destroys the brain.

That should make us all think twice.

Third, porn causes self-deception. I once heard someone say, "The problem with being deceived is you don't know that you're deceived." How true that is, especially when our behaviors turn addictive. The problem with porn is that the more one uses it the more one can't stop using it. The motto for the porn addict becomes, "Just once more." In the moment of desire he or she believes they'll be able to beat it the next time. So, in self-deceit they fulfill themselves in the moment. But the problem is they tell themselves the exact same thing the next time—and the next time, and the next time—until they really make a decision to quit viewing porn once and for all, or destroy their lives in the name of addiction.

Fourth, porn depraves the soul. Porn sucks the life out of its victims, creating within viewers an insatiable appetite that can never be satisfied and constructing an appetite that grows more deviant in what it views in order to scratch their viewing itch. If you're addicted to porn let me encourage you to get some help. ASAP. And know this: Christ can set you free (John 8:32; Philippians 4:13).

■ **Thought to Ponder**

Porn is like a cosmic vacuum cleaner. If you give yourself to it it'll suck your life away.

■ **Memory Verse**

I made a covenant with my eyes not to look lustfully at a young woman (Job 31:1).

■ **Question to Consider**

What are some other dangers of viewing porn and why should it be avoided at all costs?

■ **One-Minute Apologist Video**

Bobby Conway, "What's Wrong With Pornography?" https://www.youtube.com/watch?v=B_EDcV34SZg

Is Masturbation a Sin?

> *Masturbation is built on a self-centered view
> of sex. This wrong attitude says that sex is solely
> about you and your pleasure. Your body. Your
> genitals. Your orgasm. This is the natural tendency
> of sin. It isolates us from others and makes pleasure
> self-focused. When our lustful desires are given
> free rein, sex is pushed into a corner and made
> a completely self-centered, isolated experience
> that reinforces a self-centered view of life.*
>
> JOSHUA HARRIS

The answer to this question isn't lacking for opinions. Some people would say that masturbation is normal and amoral, while others believe masturbation is always wrong—i.e. a real moral issue.

How might we assess these various opinions?

First, as Christians we certainly wouldn't align with the view that masturbation is amoral. We may concede that it's normal, but that doesn't put it outside the question of right and wrong. Obviously, when lust enters the picture we're dealing with a real moral issue.

Some would argue that masturbation is permissible for the pubescent or pre-married individual as long as they don't lust after another person. In fact, some believe it's okay for a man to masturbate, in particular (and not to be crude) in order to release a sperm buildup, assuming he doesn't lust in the process. Obviously, there are innocent acts of masturbation for children who are in the self-discovery stage. As parents we don't want our children to think there's anything wrong with figuring out their anatomy or having a simple case of the curiosities. But that's mere child's play. And probably shouldn't even be labeled masturbation. It has nothing to do with lust because the kids I'm referring to haven't even reached puberty.

Then there are those who have reached puberty and still masturbate—even regularly. Is this wise? I don't think so. It's a little like playing with fire. Just because our body feels the need for a certain type of release doesn't mean we should cave in to our desires. As humans we have many desires in life, and nothing will erode our discipline quicker than constantly giving in to our desires. I'd rather offer my advice on the side of caution versus give a free pass in the name of some sexual release.

While I can understand how a pre-pubescent child may have innocently masturbated and even continued to do so without lusting into puberty, my fear is that if he continues with this behavior it'll only be a matter of time before he begins connecting his lusts to masturbation. When this connection feels like the perfect match, he may end up with some real challenges.

With these thoughts in mind, let me offer a few warnings.

First, realize that masturbation exhibits a lack of self-control. According to the Bible, self-control is a virtue, and is even described as a fruit of the Spirit (Galatians 5:22-23). Many people are controlled by their next episode of masturbation. Christ doesn't want us mastered by anything but Him!

Secondly, masturbation can cultivate a self-centered and pleasure-seeking appetite that warps one's view of biblical sex.

That's a frightening thought and should cause us to reserve all forms of sexual pleasure for marital love.

■ Thought to Ponder
Masturbation ultimately weakens the will, warps the mind, and wrecks one's emotions.

■ Memory Verse
This is the will of God, your sanctification: that you abstain from sexual immorality; that each one of you know how to control his own body in holiness and honor (1 Thessalonians 4:3-4).

■ Question to Consider
Do you agree with this advice regarding masturbation? If not, what good do you think can come from succumbing to masturbation?

■ One-Minute Apologist Video
Bobby Conway, "Is Masturbation a Sin?"
https://www.youtube.com/watch?v=j6U76ewB-nA

Is Drinking Alcohol a Sin?

Drink because you are happy, but never because you are miserable. Never drink when you are wretched without it, or you will be like the grey-faced gin-drinker in the slum; but drink when you would be happy without it, and you will be like the laughing peasant of Italy. Never drink because you need it, for this is rational drinking, and the way to death and hell. But drink because you do not need it, for this is irrational drinking, and the ancient health of the world.

G.K. Chesterton

The Bible isn't silent on the issue of drinking alcohol. In fact, a simple search will show you that the Scriptures are replete with advice related to alcohol. In a nutshell, the Bible doesn't condemn drinking, but it does condemn drunkenness.

In his letter to the Ephesians, Paul writes, "Do not get drunk on wine, which leads to debauchery. Instead, be filled with the Spirit" (Ephesians 5:18). Drunkenness is forbidden because it leads to a lack of self-control, foolish behavior, irresponsibility, and a life racked with consequences. Paul couldn't be clearer. He straight up warns his readers to avoid drunkenness and instead admonishes his audience to live a Spirit-controlled life.

As we consider what the Bible has to say about drinking alcohol, here are some guidelines.

First, refuse to be mastered by alcohol. If you do drink, drink moderately (1 Corinthians 6:12).

Secondly, avoid being a stumbling block to the weaker brother (see Romans 14:15-21). If you're in a situation where you can drink but you know that someone is struggling to quit drinking, avoid alcohol out of compassion for him.

Last, but not least, determine to pursue Christ as your ultimate pleasure in life (Proverbs 21:17; Philippians 1:21). Sometimes people escape to alcohol because their walk with Christ is on the lukewarm side. If you do drink, be careful to not drink as a means of escape, which can obviously lead to further problems.

I haven't had a drink since October 9, 1994, when I got clean from a hard party lifestyle. And I'm thankful that I was able to find a church and some Christian friends who were considerate of me during those early stages of sobriety. All these years later it's not a problem for me to be around alcohol. In fact, I'll even pour it for my bride, who can appreciate a glass of Pinot Grigio. The two of us are wired totally differently. I was mastered by alcohol, but Heather can drink in moderation.

So know yourself. If there's any question, I'd suggest avoiding it altogether. If you're susceptible to addiction here's one thing you can count on—you'll never be addicted if you avoid it. In the end, it's wisest to not drink, but if you do drink, drink wisely.

■ Thought to Ponder

It's one thing to enjoy alcohol in moderation and another thing to use alcohol as a form of escape.

■ **Memory Verse**

Wise is a mocker, strong drink a brawler, and whoever is led
astray by it is not wise (Proverbs 20:1).

■ **Question to Consider**

When it comes to alcohol, do you master it or does it master
you?

■ **One-Minute Apologist Video**

Bobby Conway, "Is Drinking Alcohol a Sin?"
https://www.youtube.com/watch?v=PywoFoMukog

QUESTION 10

Is It Okay to Smoke Marijuana?

Drugs will not make one's problems disappear; they will only delay the onset of having to deal with problems and will often create more problems.

SEAN MCDOWELL

In my past, I smoked plenty of marijuana, so I get the draw. Being high feels good, and when life stinks who doesn't long for a good escape? But as Christians, our escape route must look different from the non-believing world's. We are to turn toward God, not drugs. He is our pathway to freedom, unlike drugs, which often entangle us.

While the Bible speaks directly to alcohol it doesn't address the use of marijuana. Yes, I've heard the desperate attempts to justify weed usage on the basis of Genesis 1:29 where God says, "Behold, I have given you every plant yielding seed that is on the face of all the earth." But do we really think God had getting high in mind? Talk about a poor use of Scripture. And would we use the same logic for the coco leaf—the raw material for producing the drug cocaine? Of course not! We are to steward God's creation *wisely*.

Now, you might be asking, "What's wrong with smoking a little pot, especially since it's legal in certain states now?"

First, just because marijuana is legal in some states doesn't make it moral. As Christians, Scripture, not law, is to serve as our moral compass. Remember, we are to follow the law of the land so far as it aligns with our moral principles, but the moment the law conflicts with the law of God we are to side with God (Acts 4:18-19).

Second, unlike alcohol, marijuana can't be enjoyed in moderation, especially today. When I smoked weed all it took was one good hit of some green bud and one could have a pretty good high. With today's increased levels of THC the marijuana is far more potent. And while I've met countless people who can enjoy a glass of wine and be seemingly unaffected, I've never met someone in my past that smoked weed for the purpose of *not* getting high.

Third, marijuana has been medically proven to have harmful side effects—from laziness to destroying brain cells, which reduces one's IQ—two things the Bible forbids (see Proverbs 6:9-11 and 1 Corinthians 6:19-20).

Fourth, marijuana often serves as a gateway drug. It spikes one's curiosity for other drugs, leaving many wondering, "I wonder what _____ would feel like?" It has a way of capturing many of its participants and turning them into full-blown drug addicts.

With the insights provided by medical research and through examination of biblical principles, it's amazing that the question of marijuana usage is even up for debate among the Christian constituency. Avoid it, friend.

■ Thought to Ponder

Ultimate peace is never found through using drugs. It's only found through Jesus Christ.

■ Memory Verse

Training us to renounce ungodliness and worldly passions, and to live self-controlled, upright, and godly lives in the present age (Titus 2:12).

■ **Question to Consider**

Why do you think some people think that legal equals moral?

■ **One-Minute Apologist Video**

Bobby Conway, "Is It Okay to Smoke Marijuana?"
https://www.youtube.com/watch?v=cvOoTbmXfVM

Can Marijuana Be Used Medicinally?

> *I doubt that we should oppose a regulated medical use of marijuana, controlled by appropriate physician oversight and prescriptions. Many drugs are sold by prescription which, if they were abused, would be even more destructive than marijuana.*
>
> JOHN PIPER

It's no secret that many people are falsely prescribed marijuana, but is there a place for marijuana when one is truly sick? Certainly most Christians would agree that it is permissible to use certain narcotics for medicinal purposes. Studies have shown that marijuana has been useful for those struggling with cancer and may help those battling a disease to experience a relief of pain and an ability to cope with nausea and vomiting. It's also been shown to help increase one's appetite. But should this be enough for marijuana to be used legally? Let's hold that thought for now.

Here's what we do know. In the New Testament, there was an occasion where Timothy was under the weather and Paul's practical antidote was, "No longer drink only water, but use a little wine for the sake of your stomach and your frequent ailments" (1 Timothy 5:23). Note the word *little*. Even in Scripture we see alcohol prescribed to soothe Timothy's stomach issues and other ailments. With this in mind, Christians don't need to be dogmatic about the use of legally prescribed drugs if the motive is to ease one's angst. However, unless drugs are *truly* being used for medicinal purposes they should be avoided at all costs.

And herein lies the problem. Many people have abused marijuana in the name of medical help when in reality, the driving force was a desire to be high. On top of that, at least at this point, not all states allow for the use of medical marijuana. In fact, only 23 of the 50 states permit it.

If it was to be used I'd advise it to be taken in edible fashion versus inhaling, as it puts the lungs at risk. All things considered, one should think very carefully about this issue before signing off on it.

▦ Thought to Ponder

Just because something may offer a little medical reprieve doesn't mean it's holistically healthy or worth the risk.

▦ Memory Verse

Or do you not know that your body is a temple of the Holy Spirit within you, whom you have from God? You are not your own (1 Corinthians 6:19).

▦ Question to Consider

What are some other health and spiritually related issues that can surface as a result of using medical marijuana?

▦ One-Minute Apologist Video

Bobby Conway, "Can Marijuana Be Used Medicinally?" https://www.youtube.com/watch?v=ftaXHspdZBc

QUESTION 12

Is Cross-Dressing Permissible?

Cross-dressing, considered by some of little consequence today, was strictly forbidden in Israel because it obliterated the lines of distinction inherent in God's creation of man and woman.

THE APOLOGETICS STUDY BIBLE

The term often associated with a cross-dresser is *transvestite*—that is, someone who dresses opposite to his or her assigned gender. Interestingly enough, this doesn't mean that a male dressing up as a woman is a homosexual. It can, but as odd as this may sound it doesn't necessitate it. Gender issues can be very complex, and cross-dressing just adds another shade to the "fifty shades of gender" culture that we inhabit. Some people cross-dress because they don't feel their gender identity matches the gender they were assigned at birth. Others cross-dress simply as a fashion statement. They like the clothing of the opposite sex better so a guy may sport a dress or wear some high heels all in the name of "I like it."

As much as one may like the attire of the opposite sex, cross-dressing is prohibited in Scripture. The Bible says, "A woman shall not wear a man's garment, nor shall a man put on a woman's cloak, for whoever does these things is an abomination to the LORD your God" (Deuteronomy 22:5). The obvious principle that surfaces for us from this verse is that men should embrace their manhood and women should embrace their womanhood. Cross-dressing is an abomination because it is an outright rejection of God's design for us.

That's the real issue.

This verse comes from the Old Testament—from the law—but the principle hasn't rusted out with the ticking of time. In such cases, it's important to get at the principle tucked beneath the commandment. In this case, the overarching principle is that the Scriptures oppose cross-dressing because it portrays a rejection of one's divinely assigned gender (see Genesis 1:27). We are to embrace our gender. Not seek to erase it.

■ Thought to Ponder

Gender isn't a preference issue; it's a design issue.

■ Memory Verse

A woman shall not wear a man's garment, nor shall a man put on a woman's cloak, for whoever does these things is an abomination to the LORD your God (Deuteronomy 22:5).

■ Question to Consider

On one side, some may contend, "What's the big deal if a man wants to dress in women's clothing or vice versa?" How would you respond? Can you think of ways that cross-dressing can subtly loosen the moral fabric of culture?

■ One-Minute Apologist Video

Bobby Conway, "Is Cross-Dressing Permissible?"
https://www.youtube.com/watch?v=oY7v3wwVm40

Does the Bible Approve of Sex Changes?

> *Traditionally, if a man felt like a woman yet inhabited a male body, his feelings, not his body, were viewed as the problem. They were considered something to be resisted, modified if possible, and contrary to what was. Currently, what one is, is being determined by what one feels—an ominous trend when one considers its implications. It is, in essence, an attempt to define reality by desire, knowledge by intuition.*
>
> JOE DALLAS

A common complaint for someone struggling from gender identity disorder is that they feel trapped inside the wrong body. This is certainly what Bruce Jenner experienced, now referred to as Caitlyn. I can't imagine what one must feel like to have such thoughts. It truly does sound agonizing, and my heart hurts for the person experiencing such confusion. But is getting a sex change the solution? And does the Bible offer us any wisdom on the matter? Starting with the latter question, the Bible doesn't directly address this issue in the same context we understand it today, but there are some principles we can glean from Scripture.

First, gender isn't an accident—it's assigned. Genesis 1:27 says, "So God created man in his own image, in the image of God he created him; male and female he created them." What God did with Adam and Eve in assigning their gender, He's repeated with all of humanity ever since. Now you might say, "What about those born with an intersex condition whereby a person has a mixture of both male and female body parts?" This is tricky, no doubt. And a good question! I'd liken it to some of the other malfunctions that can go awry in a fallen world. Sometimes babies are born blind, without limbs, attached to their twin siblings, etc. These are all horrible and painful events that I don't want to make light of, so much so that in the event that a child is born with an intersex condition I can understand a surgery to sync up one's procreative anatomical body parts with their actual genetically revealed gender. That being said, this is a decision to approach with a lot of thought, prayer, and counsel. I also think if we are being honest, that's not really the issue in our culture today, is it? The bigger issue is people wanting to change who God made them to be.

Second, gender goes beyond our reproductive organs as our gender is expressed through the XX or XY chromosome that is inscribed through our entire cell structure. This means that even though someone may take hormonal pills or undergo a surgery for a sex change, the gender code is still evident on a cellular level, making it impossible to *actually* reverse one's inherent gender through pills and sex reassignment surgery. Consider Psalm 139:13: "For you formed my inward parts; you knitted me together in my mother's womb." While this verse says nothing about chromosomes, it certainly reveals that God is our Architect—knitting us together, even from the womb. He is the one who knit together our chromosomal structure!

Now, let's go back to the former question and ask, "Is getting a sex change the solution?" I don't think so. Not only that, getting a sex change is no guarantee that one will automatically be happy. While some may feel better, it's common knowledge that many don't and some continue to struggle with depression, identity issues, and even suicidal thoughts. It can bring on the ultimate misery when one thinks that a sex change is the end-all-be-all to self-discovery, only to realize after the surgery that life still seems beyond hopeless.

If you know some people struggling with gender identity issues, let me encourage you to struggle with them through prayer, be a sympathetic friend, help them ground their identity in Christ, encourage them to get extended counseling, and let them know that they aren't alone.

■ Thought to Ponder

The "self" that is rejected by a person obtaining a sex change is the very self that God loves and will readily receive through the gospel of Jesus Christ.

■ Memory Verse

I praise you, for I am fearfully and wonderfully made (Psalm 139:14).

■ Question to Consider

How can Christians communicate a tone of compassion for people struggling with such gender confusion without compromising their biblical convictions?

■ One-Minute Apologist Video

Bobby Conway, "Does the Bible Approve of Sex Changes?" https://www.youtube.com/watch?v=uaJw3v_5tkY

Who Is the Trinity?

> *Some Jews and Muslims accuse Christians*
> *of being idolatrous for believing in the*
> *Trinity. My response to both groups is that*
> *they fundamentally misunderstand the*
> *Christian understanding of the Trinity.*
>
> MIROSLAV VOLF

In short, the Trinity is God. Yet many have falsely assumed that Christians believe in three gods. Such is the misdirected view of many Muslims, Jews, and Jehovah's Witnesses. That would be tritheism—a slimmed-down version of polytheism. Christians aren't tritheists. They're monotheists who believe in one God revealed in three Persons: Father, Son, and Holy Spirit. Think of it like this: There's one "what" and three "who's." There's one what— God. And three who's— the Father, Son, and Holy Spirit.

For obvious reasons this has caused great consternation for many thinkers. Some even conclude that the Christian view of the Trinity is a contradiction. At first sight this may seem to be the case, but it's not. Remember, Christians aren't claiming that God is three persons revealed in one person or one God in three gods, rather Christians believe there is one God revealed in three Persons. See the difference?

Perhaps I can illustrate. But not without warning. Illustrations of the Trinity are far from perfect. Almost all quickly break down, even into heresy. No illustration can perfectly depict God, but illustrations can help us grasp God's three and oneness. For example, the Trinity is not 1+1+1 = 3, but 1x1x1 = 1. Or consider that a single triangle has three sides. Such illustrations help us to see how something can be three and one, but they can become very unhelpful when they move beyond that.

In conclusion, Christians aren't tritheists, their view of the Trinity isn't a contradiction, and Christians must be cautious using illustrations to depict the Trinity. And at the same time, Christians can worship both the clarity and the mystery of their Triune God.

■ Thought to Ponder

The doctrine of the Trinity has mystified both children and scholars alike.

■ Memory Verse

The grace of the Lord Jesus Christ and the love of God and the fellowship of the Holy Spirit be with you all (2 Corinthians 13:14).

■ Question to Consider

What are some illustrations people use to explain the Trinity that actually teach heresy?

■ One-Minute Apologist Video

Brett Kunkle, "Is the Trinity Unscriptural and Unreasonable?" https://www.youtube.com/watch?v=5NuKvP81hSQ

What Is Modalism?

> *During the third century, a heresy arose which*
> *is called "Modalism" or "Sabellianism" or*
> *"Monarchianism." According to this heresy, the*
> *Father, the Son, and the Holy Spirit are all*
> *divine, but they are not distinct persons.*
>
> WILLIAM LANE CRAIG

Modalism is a heresy that denies the doctrine of the Trinity. Often surprising to some Christians, United Pentecostals ascribe to this ancient heresy. Modalism teaches that God is a single person who has eternally existed and yet He has revealed Himself in three modes, or forms.

Modalism rejects the Trinitarian belief that God exists at all times as three distinct Persons—Father, Son, and Holy Spirit. Rather, the modalist believes that God is one person made known in three modes. In the Old Testament, God manifested Himself in the mode of the Father. With the incarnation, God manifested Himself in the mode of the Son. Following Jesus's ascension, God made Himself known through the mode of the Holy Spirit. Problematically, modalism rejects that the Father, Son, and Holy Spirit exist *simultaneously*, which means that modalists deny the distinctiveness of the three Persons in the Trinity.

This problem is compounded when you consider the baptism of Jesus. At His baptism, we see all three Persons of the Trinity present. The Father speaks from heaven, the Son is baptized, and the

Spirit descends upon Jesus like a dove (see Matthew 3:16-17). Furthermore, after His resurrection Jesus told His disciples to baptize people in the Name of the Father, Son, and Holy Spirit (Matthew 28:19). New converts were to be baptized in the One Name (i.e. God) who exists in three Persons (namely the Father, Son, and Holy Spirit).

The problem is obvious—to embrace modalism is to reject the Trinity.

And to reject the Trinity is to reject orthodox Christianity.

▨ Thought to Ponder

Modalism rejects Trinitarianism for a more nuanced form of Unitarianism.

▨ Memory Verse

The grace of the Lord Jesus Christ and the love of God and the fellowship of the Holy Spirit be with you all (2 Corinthians 13:14).

▨ Question to Consider

What difference does it make if all three Persons of the Trinity don't simultaneously exist?

▨ One-Minute Apologist Video

Bobby Conway, "What Is Modalism?"
https://www.youtube.com/watch?v=KMPIxCDDxTs

Is Jesus God?

*I am trying here to prevent anyone saying the really
foolish thing that people often say about Him: I'm
ready to accept Jesus as a great moral teacher, but
I don't accept his claim to be God. That is the one
thing we must not say. A man who was merely a
man and said the sort of things Jesus said would
not be a great moral teacher. He would either be
a lunatic—on the level with the man who says he
is a poached egg—or else he would be the Devil of
Hell. You must make your choice. Either this man
was, and is, the Son of God, or else a madman or
something worse. You can shut him up for a fool,
you can spit at him and kill him as a demon or
you can fall at his feet and call him Lord and God,
but let us not come with any patronizing nonsense
about his being a great human teacher. He has
not left that open to us. He did not intend to.*

C.S. Lewis

There is more confusion around the person of Jesus Christ than
any other figure in human history. While most people readily
accept that Jesus was a man, many will rage if you claim that He is
more than a man.

But was He?

And if so, what's the evidence?

First, Jesus understood Himself to be divine. He claimed to be the eternal Yahweh (John 8:58). He claimed equality with God (John 5:18; 10:30). He openly accepted worship (Matthew 8:2; 9:18; 14:33; 15:31; Mark 5:6; John 9:38; 20:28). He forgave sin (Matthew 9:2; Luke 7:47-48; John 8:11). He even expected His disciples to pray in His name (John 14:13-14).

Second, the disciples believed Jesus was divine. Thomas called Him God (John 20:28). John wrote, "In the beginning was the word, and the word was with God, and the word was God" (John 1:1). Matthew referred to Jesus as "Immanuel," which means "God with us" (Matthew 1:23). Paul wrote of Jesus, "For in him the whole fullness of deity dwells bodily" (Colossians 2:9). And that is just a mere sampling.

Third, God the Father recognized the divinity of Christ. In Hebrews 1:8 we read, "Of the Son [God] says, 'Your throne, O God, is forever and ever.'" In this verse the Father is calling Jesus, His Son, God. Pretty powerful!

Finally, the early church believed Jesus was divine. This is seen through their writings and creedal documents such as the Nicene and Chalcedonian Creeds. For example, the Chalcedonian Creed of 451 exclaims that Jesus is "truly God and truly man." That is to say that He's one person with two natures: human and divine. He's man and He's more than a man. He's the God-man.

That's the story of Jesus.

His disciples.

The Father.

And church history.

It's our story too, Christian.

▓ Thought to Ponder
Jesus is more than a man.

▓ Memory Verse
We wait for the blessed hope—the appearing of the glory of our great God and Savior Jesus Christ (Titus 2:13).

▓ Question to Consider
What's at stake if we relegate Jesus to being merely a man?

▓ One-Minute Apologist Video
J. Warner Wallace, "Did Jesus Think Jesus Was God?"
https://www.youtube.com/watch?v=gHFecSfT9CI

Does John 1:1 Teach That Jesus Was God *or* "a" god?

> *No matter how far back we may try to push our imagination, we can never reach a point at which we could say of the Divine Word, as Arius did, "There was once when he was not."*
>
> F.F. BRUCE

One of the most theologically in-depth passages in all Scripture is John 1:1. It's a verse you could quickly coast over if you weren't privy to all that's entailed within this morsel of truth. This verse is a Christian gem. Frankly, it's stunning how much truth can be embedded in such a few words. John 1:1 is that way. It's economical in word use and explosive with exegesis.

This verse says, "In the beginning was the word and the word was with God and the word was God." The trigger word is *Word*. It's the Greek word "logos," which serves as a title referring to Jesus. The Logos is God's quintessential self-unveiling of Himself to mankind in the Person of Jesus Christ. How does John 1:1 help us understand that Jesus, the Word, is divine?

First, John 1:1 reveals that the Word was eternal. John 1:1 says, "In the beginning *was* the word." The word *was* is featured in the imperfect tense, indicating a *continued* existence. So we can unpack it as follows. The word, the eternal logos, Jesus Christ, was *already* in the beginning before the beginning became a beginning.

Before time began the Word was *already* existing—eternally existing. He was there before all of this (creation) was here.

Second, John 1:1 calls the Word *God*. Now John takes us deeper into the theology of the eternal logos by attributing deity to Jesus Christ. In the final part of the verse he writes, "And the Word was with God, and the word was God." So we see that Jesus was not only with God, but *is* God. This is one of those verses that helps us see the plurality within the Godhead. We believe there is one God revealed in three separate Persons: Father, Son, and Holy Spirit.

This is important, especially when dealing with Jehovah's Witnesses who misconstrue John 1:1 in their New World Translation. Their version reads, "And the word was a god." Notice, not *God* but *a god*. Why is this? There is no definite article ("the") in the Greek, so they've put in an indefinite article ("a"). Jehovah's Witnesses hope to get around Jesus's deity by translating John 1:1 as such. Now, it's not that they're slipping into full-born polytheism by claiming He was "*a* god," but they want to say something like, "He was godlike." Jehovah's Witnesses are monotheists. To them, Jesus was the first *created* being, not an *uncreated* being.

How can we reply to a Jehovah's Witness? It's not necessary to translate Greek nouns lacking an article as indefinite. Even Jehovah's Witnesses aren't consistent here. Rather, their use of the article is used or not used when it's convenient to fit their theology. If they were consistent in their New World Translation they'd have to utilize "a" before God in several other spots, even within John 1. For example, what do verses 6, 12, 13, and 18 in this chapter have in common? They're all missing a definite article in the Greek before the word "God." If they were to translate the aforementioned verses as indefinite, here's how they would read:

• "There came a man who was sent from *a* God" (John 1:6).

- "He gave the right to become Children of *a* God" (John 1:12).

- "Who were born...of *a* God" (John 1:13).

- "No one has ever seen *a* God" (John 1:18).

As you can see, this would be a theological game changer. Jehovah's Witnesses aren't facing the facts. And the fact is, Jesus is divine. He's God in the flesh. Here's a clear example of where cultic apologetics are won or lost in the Greek. The original languages don't reveal a Jesus who is a god. Rather, they reveal a Jesus who is God. It's not the article (necessarily) that determines the translation of the word. It's the context. Once Jesus becomes anything less than fully God and fully man, we've become a cult. Next time you talk to a Jehovah's Witness, remember that words matter, especially when talking about the *Word*.

■ Thought to Ponder

The battle for truth is often won or lost in the original languages.

■ Memory Verse

In the beginning was the Word, and the Word was with God, and the Word was God (John 1:1).

■ Question to Consider

How well does your church equip its members to understand the importance of theological doctrine?

■ One-Minute Apologist Video

Bobby Conway, "How Do Jehovah's Witnesses Interpret John 1:1?"

https://www.youtube.com/watch?v=Q5x2KGF7XbU

Could Jesus Have Sinned?

> *If we are asking if it was actually possible for Jesus to have sinned, it seems that we must conclude that it was not possible. The union of his human and divine natures in one person prevented it.*
>
> WAYNE GRUDEM

Do the terms *peccability* and *impeccability* mean anything to you? Perhaps not! And that's okay. Theologians use these two terms to describe Jesus's ability to sin or not to sin.

Those who hold to the peccability view believe that Jesus could've sinned, but didn't. Those who believe that Jesus was impeccable also believe that He didn't sin, but they take it one step further and say He *couldn't* have sinned. He's impeccable.

And therein lies the debate, leaving the question, "Could Jesus have sinned?" begging for resolve. Again, note the point of agreement between the two views. Jesus *didn't* sin. But *could* He have? Hebrews 4:15 says, "We do not have a high priest who is unable to sympathize with our weaknesses, but one who in every respect has been tempted as we are, yet without sin."

A person who believes Jesus could have sinned might argue, "How could Jesus have been tempted in all our ways if He wasn't truly able to sin?" Fair question. Though it's not as hard to answer as some might think. For example, consider this question: Can an undefeatable army still be attacked? Of course! In the same way,

Jesus could have felt the force of temptation without the ability to succumb to it.

In reality, to believe in the doctrine of peccability poses a deeper theological problem. Here's why. One must remember that Jesus has two natures: a human nature and a divine nature.

Let me illustrate. Suppose I handed you an iron hanger—could you bend it? Obviously, it doesn't take Popeye to do that. It requires no spinach. But suppose I handed you a crowbar. Could you bend that? No way—even if you just consumed a spinach buffet the bar would remain unbendable. Now if you took the iron hanger and wrapped it around the crowbar, could you still bend the iron hanger? No, because the hanger is now connected to the crowbar.

In this example, the iron hanger represents Christ's human nature and the crowbar depicts Christ's divine nature. Since Jesus had a human nature He could experience the full force of being tempted, but because He had a divine nature He was protected from falling into temptation, therefore remaining impeccable. His divine nature overrode His human nature. Aren't you grateful for that? I am.

Here's the real problem with the doctrine of peccability. *God can't act contrary to His nature.* That's a biggie. It's impossible for God to sin. God can't do what is logically impossible. He can't draw a square circle. He can't cease to be God. He can't become me. Nor can He become you. And He can't make a rock so big that He cannot lift it. These issues don't pose problems. They may pose a little thinking, but not a problem. A holy God can't sin. Impossible.

Interestingly enough, in one sense Jesus's divine nature couldn't even be tempted. As James wrote, "God cannot be tempted with evil" (James 1:13) and in another sense His human nature could be and was (Luke 4:2). Since Jesus was *God* in the flesh He couldn't have sinned, but since Jesus was in the *flesh* He could be tempted. That's worth chewing on.

▦ Thought to Ponder

Jesus experienced the force of temptation and triumphed without sin.

▦ Memory Verse

He committed no sin, neither was deceit found in his mouth (1 Peter 2:22).

▦ Question to Consider

What's at stake if it was possible for Jesus to sin?

▦ One-Minute Apologist Video

Bobby Conway, "Could Jesus Have Sinned?"
https://www.youtube.com/watch?v=1Bao2whWL1A

Does Prophecy Confirm Jesus as Messiah?

So important is prediction to the very nature of the Bible that it is estimated that it involves 27 percent of the Bible. God certainly is the Lord of the future.

WALTER C. KAISER, JR.

It's often been stated that the Old Testament contains some three hundred prophecies that Jesus fulfilled during His coming. The precise number varies among scholars, but the number is huge.

To help understand the significance of Jesus's fulfillment of these prophecies, Peter Stoner offers this widely known example in his book *Science Speaks*. To be especially conservative, Stoner calculated the chances of Jesus fulfilling only eight prophecies. Stoner claims that the odds of this happening are 1 in 10^{17} power. That would be 1 chance in 100,000,000,000,000,000 (17 zeros after the one). That's a number so mind-boggling that it's impossible to grasp apart from an illustration.

Stoner provides one by having us envision 10^{17} silver dollars spread out over the entire state of Texas. The amount is so vast that the silver dollars would cover the state of Texas two feet deep. Now mark one of the silver dollars and stir them all up. Then blindfold a man and let him know that he can go wherever he wishes, but he's only allowed to pick one silver dollar out of the entire mass of silver dollars covering the state of Texas. What are the chances of him picking up the marked silver dollar? The same chance that the prophets had of writing out just *eight* prophecies that would be actualized in Jesus. Astonishing! If that's not convincing, I'm not sure what is.

This not only validates Jesus as the Messiah, but it also gives credence to the credibility of God's inspired Word (Matthew 5:17). If the odds of fulfilling eight prophecies seem staggering, imagine the math on roughly three hundred prophecies.

■ Thought to Ponder

A great way to put doubt to rest is to ponder the odds of fulfilled prophecy in Scripture.

■ Memory Verse

Do not think that I have come to abolish the Law or the Prophets; I have not come to abolish them but to fulfill them (Matthew 5:17).

■ Question to Consider

How can learning some of these prophecies both encourage your faith and make you more effective in sharing the gospel with nonbelievers?

■ One-Minute Apologist Video

Bobby Conway, "Does Prophecy Confirm Jesus Is the Messiah?" https://www.youtube.com/watch?v=pVSqxVV0WgM

What Does *Begotten* Mean?

> We believe in one Lord, Jesus Christ, the
> only Son of God, eternally begotten of the
> Father, God from God, Light from Light, true
> God from true God, begotten, not made.
>
> THE NICENE CREED

Begotten. Not a word we use every day. And it certainly didn't make the trending words list this year. Nevertheless, this word is theologically dense. It's packed full of doctrinal insight. In what is perhaps the most famous verse in all Scripture, we read, "For God so loved the world, that he gave his only begotten Son, that whoever believes in him should not perish but have everlasting life" (John 3:16 NKJV). Many, like myself, hear the word *begotten* for the first time and think, "What does that mean?"

And how one defines this word will say a lot about who they understand Jesus to be. It's a word we can't afford to misinterpret as many false teachers have done. There have been numerous wolves in sheep clothing that misconstrued *begotten*, and as a result they've heretically emptied Jesus of His divinity.

So what does *begotten* mean? In its literal sense, *begotten* refers to a child who shares the same nature as his father. False teachers have taught that the word means produced, made, or created. But think about it. If Jesus was produced, made, or created, He's not divine. This is crucial. If words matter—and they do—then rarely has a word mattered more.

This word powerfully shows that Jesus shares the same *divine* nature as the Father. Begotten is meant to equate Jesus with the Father, not deflate Him before the Father. In *Mere Christianity*, C.S. Lewis colors this word for us by illustrating what *begotten* means:

> When you beget, you beget something of the same kind as yourself. A man begets human babies, a beaver begets little beavers and a bird begets eggs, which turn into little birds. But when you make, you make something of a different kind from yourself. A bird makes a nest, a beaver builds a dam, a man makes a wireless set—or he may make something more like himself than a wireless set: say, a statue. If he is a clever enough carver he may make a statue, which is very like man indeed. But, of course, it is not a real man; it only looks like one. It cannot breathe or think. It is not alive.
>
> Now that is the first thing to get clear. What God begets is God; just as what man begets is man. What God creates is not God; just as what man makes is not man. That is why men are not Sons of God in the sense that Christ is. They may be like God in certain ways, but they are not things of the same kind. They are more like statues or pictures of God.

Well said.

Jesus's divine nature has been defended since the early church. In the fourth century a teacher named Arius taught that Jesus was a created being and refused to embrace the divinity of Christ. Emperor Constantine called together a group of bishops at Nicea to settle the Arian controversy once and for all. By the end of the council, the bishops had formulated a creed that rejected Arianism by strongly affirming that Jesus was "begotten, not made." This

wonderfully worded creed was meant to state with precision that
Jesus Christ is Immanuel. God with us!

Thought to Ponder

Jesus eternally existed as God before He ever existed in human
flesh.

Memory Verse

For God so loved the world, that he gave his only Son, that
whoever believes in him should not perish but have eternal life
(John 3:16).

Question to Consider

What difference would it make to your Christian life if Jesus
weren't divine?

One-Minute Apologist Video

Bobby Conway, "What Does Begotten Mean?"
https://www.youtube.com/watch?v=wSWkWGu-_rE

Who Is the Holy Spirit?

> *The Spirit is both the interior expression
> of the unseen God's personality and the
> visible manifestation of God's activity in the
> world. The Spirit is truly God in action.*
>
> GORDON D. FEE

If you want to liven up the conversation with a group of strangers just pose the question, "Who is the Holy Spirit?" That ought to make for an interesting conversation. It's probably no surprise to you that there's a lot of abuse done in the name of the Holy Spirit—even within the church. At one end of the spectrum you've got the Spirit-*phobia* crowd, and on the other end there's the Spirit-*mania* groupies. And here's the common denominator: both operate in the extremes. One group is afraid to see the Spirit work through anything and the other group sees the Spirit working through *everything*. These two extremes have caused some people to check out of the conversation altogether and simply plead ignorance. Sort of like the child who referred to God as the Father, the Son, and the *Other One*.

But is the Spirit unknowable? Is He pure conundrum? Or can we elucidate some of the enigma? Can we make sense of some of the mystery?

I think we can.

To do so, let's go back to where we began by asking, "Who

is the Holy Spirit?" Some don't ask who; they ask what. That is the case with Jehovah's Witnesses. To them, the Holy Spirit isn't a *Who* but a powerful *What*—a life force, not a person, and most certainly not God. But as Christians, we believe the Holy Spirit is a *Who*. And who is He? He's the third person of the Trinity. He's God the Spirit.

Now you might ask, "How is it that Christians understand the Holy Spirit to be personal?" The Scriptures speak of Him as such. For example, the Holy Spirit can be lied to (Acts 5:3), resisted (Acts 7:51), grieved (Ephesians 4:30), quenched (1 Thessalonians 5:19), blasphemed (Mark 3:29), outraged (Hebrews 10:29), and much more. A force can't be affected that way. Now, don't confuse person with human. The Holy Spirit is a *divine Person* whereas we are *human persons*. And by person, I'm not speaking bodily. The Holy Spirit is immaterial. He's Spirit. By person, I'm speaking *relationally*. God the Spirit is a relational God. And like us, as a personal God He has mind, will, and emotions (though some philosophers would argue whether God can emote). When the Bible speaks of the Holy Spirit, it doesn't refer to the Holy Spirit as an "it"; rather the Scriptures use the personal pronouns *he*, *his*, and *him* (for example, see John 16:7-15).

But not only is the Holy Spirit a person, He's a *divine* person. He's the third person of the Trinity (Matthew 28:19; 2 Corinthians 13:14). He has all the divine attributes of God the Father and God the Son. The Bible depicts the Holy Spirit as all-powerful (Luke 1:35), ever-present (Psalm 139:7-8) and all-knowing (1 Corinthians 2:10-11). And to top it all off, His name is Holy.

That's who the Holy Spirit is in crash course fashion. Call it Holy Spirit 101.

Thought to Ponder

The Holy Spirit is not a person-less object to be analyzed, but a personal Subject to be adored.

Memory Verse

Go therefore and make disciples of all nations, baptizing them in the name of the Father and of the Son and of the Holy Spirit (Matthew 28:19).

Question to Consider

If you were to err on the side of Spirit-phobia or Spirit-mania, where would you lean and why?

One-Minute Apologist Video

Jason Jimenez, "Who Is the Holy Spirit?"
www.youtube.com/watch?v=7L8A00LRg-Q

What Is the Role of the Holy Spirit?

> *You might as well try to see without eyes, hear*
> *without ears, or breathe without lungs as to try to*
> *live the Christian life without the Holy Spirit.*
>
> D.L. MOODY

A.W. Tozer, a twentieth-century spiritual sage, famously said, "If the Holy Spirit was withdrawn from the church today, 95 percent of what we do would go on and no one would know the difference." Can you say, "Ouch"? Talk about a scary thought. Tozer seems to be on to something here. He recognized what many Christians today fail to recognize—the role of the Holy Spirit. The early church knew what the Holy Spirit was up to and the importance of recognizing His role in the church. But does today's church at large have this sense? No, says Tozer. And I'm inclined to agree.

This lack of understanding isn't because the Bible is thin on content. No, the curious Christian is amply supplied with material about the Holy Spirit. Let's take a brief look at what the Scripture has to say regarding the role of the Holy Spirit in the believer's life.

It is the Holy Spirit who convicts us of our sins (John 16:8). He's the one who sheds light on our conscience when each of us falls short of God's glory. Furthermore, the Holy Spirit's role is vital in bringing nonbelievers to salvation (Titus 3:5). So much so that no one is saved apart from the work of the Spirit. If you're a

Christian, it's because you've *already* experienced the work of the Holy Spirit in your life.

But there's more. The work of God's Spirit is *ongoing*. Once we're saved, the Holy Spirit provides us with assurance of our salvation (Romans 8:16). As Christians, we are fortunate. That's because the Holy Spirit comes bearing gifts—spiritual gifts (1 Corinthians 12:11). Our spiritual gifts are given to us to be a source of blessing and encouragement to others. They come tethered with a purpose. It's hard to fulfill God's will if you haven't unwrapped the gift(s) He's given you to help fulfill it. Thankfully, we aren't left to our own strength after we become Christians. Here's what happens.

The Holy Spirit is there for us to both empower and fill us with His presence so that we can make the most our lives (Romans 8:11; Ephesians 5:18). Trying to fulfill the Christian life in our own strength will only serve as a lesson in futility. The Holy Spirit is passionate about producing spiritual fruit in our lives. This fruit represents Christlike character. In his letter to the Galatians, Paul writes, "But the fruit of the Spirit is love, joy, peace, patience, kindness, goodness, faithfulness, gentleness, self-control; against such things there is no law" (Galatians 5:22-23).

Now go back over what I just wrote and ask yourself, "Where can I cooperate more with the Holy Spirit in my life?" Paul admonishes us, "If we live by the Spirit, let us also keep in step with the Spirit" (Galatians 5:25). Learn what the role of the Holy Spirit is, and then watch the difference He can make in your life.

■ Thought to Ponder

Trying to live the Christian life apart from the Holy Spirit is as senseless as trying to iron a shirt without plugging the iron into the outlet. As Christians, we need to get plugged in.

■ Memory Verse

When the Spirit of truth comes, he will guide you into all the truth, for he will not speak on his own authority, but whatever he hears he will speak, and he will declare to you the things that are to come (John 16:13).

■ Question to Consider

Do you sense the Holy Spirit at work in your life? If so, how?

■ One-Minute Apologist Video

Bobby Conway, "What Is the Role of the Holy Spirit in Our Life?"
www.youtube.com/watch?v=EVEz026Jg-U

How Do I Discover
My Spiritual Gifts?

*I admit then that the society of the godly cannot
exist, except when each one is content with his
own measure, and imparts to others the gifts
which he has received, and allows himself by
turns to be assisted by the gifts of others.*

JOHN CALVIN

I'm not sure how you open gifts at Christmas time, but our family's custom was to first open the presents under the tree and then afterward we could discover what was in our stockings. Spiritual gifts are like stocking stuffers—the added gifts that come subsequent to God's greatest gift, our salvation. Spiritual gifts are like the ice cream on your apple pie or the icing on your cake. God generously tops off our salvation by gifting His church for the purpose of building it up and reaching the world.

As a pastor, I've had many people ask me through the years, "How do I discover my spiritual gifts?" This is an important question. No magic formula exists for discovering your spiritual gifts, but here are a few suggestions worth pondering.

First, study what the Bible says about spiritual gifts. As you dig into New Testament passages such as Romans 12:4-8, 1 Corinthians 12, and 1 Peter 4:10-11, you'll notice that there are a variety of gifts. However, these lists aren't exhaustive but exemplary. They're designed to show you *some* of the gifts but not *all* of the gifts.

Second, pay close attention to your burdens. You'll often discover your gift behind your burden. The evangelist is burdened to see nonbelievers saved. The leader is burdened to see change. The encourager wants people to feel hope. So ask yourself, "What am I burdened about?" The answer may be the secret to unwrapping your spiritual gift.

Third, prayerfully ask God to show how He's gifted you. Commune with God. But as you seek Him be careful to not slip into a user relationship. Many people get so consumed with seeking their spiritual gifts that they fail to seek the Giver of the gifts. Chase His heart, not His hand. There's a big difference. We don't want to use God; we want to be used by Him.

Fourth, make sure you're seeking to live a biblically aligned life. Many Christians want God to reveal their spiritual gifts to them, but they aren't interested in following Him. This is odd. Gifts aren't given to increase our glory; they're given to make known God's glory.

Fifth, start serving anywhere and everywhere. Where there is a need, seek to fill it. I played baseball growing up, and I learned that if you're going to find your sweet spot, you've got to try out different positions. Eventually, it becomes clear what position to play. So too in the church, don't wait for some mystical vision or dream to happen. Get busy. Start serving. And eventually you'll find your sweet spot.

Sixth, ask those who know you, "How do you think God has gifted me?" We can gather some great wisdom from those who watch our lives up close. I'm sure you've got some friends who would gladly offer you some sound advice, especially if they've got the gift of encouragement. That's what God-gifted encouragers do—they call out the gifts in others. Yet, sometimes in their desire to encourage, they may not be as constructive with their advice. So be discerning.

Seventh, take a spiritual gift inventory test. You can find these online or elsewhere. These tests will vary as some have differing opinions about which gifts are active today. For example, some Christians believe gifts like healing, tongues, and prophecy are no longer in operation whereas others do. Their view of such gifts will determine how the inventory test is developed. I encourage you to ask your pastor if he has any suggestions, and then study up.

■ Thought to Ponder

One of life's great satisfactions is using your gifts to glorify God and serve others.

■ Memory Verse

Now concerning spiritual gifts, brothers, I do not want you to be uninformed (1 Corinthians 12:1).

■ Question to Consider

Have you discovered your spiritual gift(s)? If so, what are they?

■ One-Minute Apologist Video

Bobby Conway, "How Do I Discover My Spiritual Gifts?"
www.youtube.com/watch?v=a6QgkYhEafM

How Do I Study the Bible?

*Bible study is like eating peanuts. The
more you eat, the more you want to eat.*

PAUL LITTLE

A wise man once said, "Give a man a fish and you'll feed him a meal. Teach a man to fish and you'll feed him for a lifetime." I've always resonated with that statement. And such a quip applies directly to studying the Bible. Many people are content to depend on others for their spiritual meals, but in a culture like ours, where the Bible is readily available and there are so many tools at our disposal, there is no excuse for Christians to not know the skill of preparing their own scriptural meals. This isn't to shun teachers. We should all be learning from gifted teachers. But we should also be learning the art of Bible study for ourselves.

During my time at Dallas Theological Seminary, I had the privilege to take Bible study methods (aka hermeneutics) under Howard Hendricks, affectionately referred to as "Prof." He structured his course around three primary words: *observation*, *interpretation*, and *application*. When studying the Bible, if you can grasp these three words, you'll be well on your way to becoming a better student of Scripture.

First, let's consider *the observation stage*. Observation seeks to answer the question, "What do I see?" It's been said the difference between a good student and a bad student of Scripture is simple—the good student simply *sees* more. He's developed his observation skills. The psalmist was mindful of this, saying, "Open my eyes, that I may behold wondrous things out of your law" (Psalm 119:18).

To help us develop our observation skills, Prof had us read Acts 1:8 and write down twenty-five observations. Once we finished this agonizing task, we turned the assignment in only to have him hand it back and say, "Now go make twenty-five more." What was he doing? He was increasing our observation skills. Imagine that—fifty observations from one verse.

Now, you might ask, "What are we *looking* for?" That's a great question. I developed an acrostic to help you navigate the observation stage. Here it is:

> **O**bserve prayerfully.
> **B**egin your study by seeing the big picture.
> **S**elect key word(s).
> **E**xplore any commands to follow.
> **R**ecord any warnings given.
> **V**enture to find the promises proclaimed.
> **A**sk and answer questions that are naturally raised in the text.
> **T**arget key people and places.
> **I**nspect for contrasts and comparisons.
> **O**verview your discoveries in light of the broader context.
> **N**ote words that are repeated and emphasized.
> **S**elect the style of literature (e.g., apocalyptic, poetic, historical).

Once you've completed your thorough observations of a passage, you're ready to move to the *interpretation stage.* I cannot stress it enough that we aren't in a position to provide an interpretation until we first complete the observation stage. *Observation prepares the way for interpretation.*

Paul exhorts us in 2 Timothy 2:15, "Do your best to present yourself to God as one approved, a worker who has no need to be ashamed, rightly handling the word of truth." Though Paul was addressing Timothy as a pastor charged with teaching the Word, we too must seek to accurately handle Scripture.

The question we are seeking to answer in interpretation is, *"What does the text mean?"* I encourage you at this stage to read your passage in several different translations. Furthermore, be sure to purchase a good Bible dictionary, a Bible atlas, a Bible handbook, some commentaries covering the book you're studying, and a concordance. All of these tools combined will enable you to get at the author's intended meaning, which is the key to interpretation. If you're a software junkie and don't want to deal with a bunch of books, check out the resources provided by Logos Bible Software at www.logos.com.

At last, once you've made observations leading you to a proper interpretation, you're now ready to enter the *application stage*. There's one interpretation (from God's perspective) and many applications. Application is crucial. Through application we build a bridge from the ancient text to our current context. Application asks the question, *"How does it work?"*

James the apostle was a great pragmatician. He said, "But don't just listen to God's word. You must do what it says. Otherwise, you are only fooling yourselves" (James 1:22, NLT). Prof told us about a student who said to him, "I've been through the Bible twelve times." Prof replied, "That's great. But the real question is, how many times has the Bible been through you?"

Next time you study your Bible, try this three-staged approach and never forget that the Bible is meant to be more than studied—it's meant to be *lived*.

■ Thought to Ponder

We need to approach the Bible the way a doctor approaches his patient. First he asks some observation questions before he interprets what's wrong. Once the diagnosis has been made, he's now ready to provide an application (a course of treatment).

■ Memory Verse

Open my eyes, that I may behold wondrous things out of your law (Psalm 119:18).

■ Question to Consider

What would you think of a doctor if you walked into his office and he handed you a prescription without first assessing your condition?

■ One-Minute Apologist Video

Bobby Conway, "How to Develop an Appetite for Bible Study," www.youtube.com/watch?v=lbUwasudt70

Can We Adapt the Bible to Our Tastes?

*The Bible will keep you from sin, or
sin will keep you from the Bible.*

D.L. MOODY

When it comes to the Bible, we live in a buffet culture whereby people pick and choose what they like and disregard what they don't. But we can't chew the meat and spit out the bones as it relates to God's Word. We do not have the right to shun *or* switch up something to fit our tastes.

If you've read the Bible long enough, you have doubtlessly come across a passage that was hard to digest. It may be a passage about sin, repentance, judgment, suffering, wrath, or even hell. Here is the key: if deep in our hearts we have a distaste for something in God's Word, such as the doctrine of sin, we don't have the right to change the Bible to make it more digestible. Our duty is to align ourselves with God's Word, not make it align with our preferences. Our job is to ask, "What does the Bible say?" not "What do I want it to say?"

When something about God's Word is less than flavorful to us, we must realize that *we* are the problem, not God. Our responsibility is not to change God (He is immutable) or to create God in our own image, but to explore our hearts to discover *why* we are resisting His Word. When our emotions are at odds with a theological truth, we must resist the temptation to water down the Scriptures in the name of soothing our emotions. Rather, we must see this as a sanctification issue and ask ourselves, "Why do my emotions resist this theological truth?"

The answer will often be quite revealing.

Next time you struggle swallowing a portion of Scripture, ask yourself: "Deep down do I struggle with the justice of God? Have I lost sight of God's incomprehensible holiness? Am I blinded to the depth of my own depravity? Do I trust that God is simultaneously just *and* loving?"

Remember, it's the hard portions that often reveal our heart problems. It's often the things we wrestle with the most that disclose the hidden character flaws we battle most intensely. Ultimately, it comes down to trust. Do we trust the nature of God and believe that He is good? If so, that can help us to move confidently through the not-so-tasty portions of Scripture.

▪ Thought to Ponder

Our job is to conform to Scripture rather than make it conform to us.

▪ Memory Verse

Give me understanding, that I may keep your law and observe it with my whole heart (Psalm 119:34).

▪ Question to Consider

What parts of the Bible do you find yourself seeking to water down?

▪ One-Minute Apologist Video

Bobby Conway, "Can We Adapt the Bible to Fit Our Taste?" www.youtube.com/watch?v=kxTfwdPGKMY

How Should a Christian Vote?

> *If we don't make ourselves heard, the consequences will be grave—not just for us, but for our fellow citizens. Like it or not, in a free society, we're God's agents for picking righteous, able men and women.*
>
> CHARLES COLSON

Voting is a privilege that each of us *gets* to exercise in this great democracy. But it's critical that we cast an informed vote. Here are six tips to remember before entering the voting booth.

First, remember that no one enters the voting booth alone. As Christians, we should ask, "If Jesus were voting in this election, how would He vote?" We should seek to vote how we can best envision Jesus voting. It adds a little weight to our vote if we can remember that Jesus goes into the booth with us. He said, "I am with you always" (Matthew 28:20). As an ever-present Savior, Jesus is aware of the decisions we make. Our aim should be to represent His values to the best of our ability. We shouldn't leave our Christianity outside the voting booth.

Second, remember that no matter who rules the earth, God still rules the universe. This principle is so encouraging because it reminds us that ultimately God is still in control. Proverbs 21:1 says, "The king's heart is a stream of water in the hand of the LORD; he turns it wherever he will." We can take comfort knowing that God will accomplish His purposes on earth regardless of who's in office. God will not be caught by surprise on voting day, and He certainly will not throw His hands up in the air in defeat. Therefore, we don't need to be alarmists, but we can rest in God's sovereign plans. No matter how bad things get, we can say with confidence, "Our God reigns."

Third, remember to vote on principles over personality. Principles trump personality. The election isn't a personality contest. It's more like a principle contest. Our voting motto could be, "He who has the best principles wins." As followers of Christ, we should vote for the person whose values best reflect our biblical worldview. Our vote should be biblically measured.

Fourth, remember to enter the voting booth prayerfully and to pray for your leaders continuously. Paul the apostle instructed young Timothy by writing, "First of all, then, I urge that supplications, prayers, intercessions, and thanksgivings be made for all people, for kings and all who are in high positions, that we may lead a peaceful and quiet life, godly and dignified in every way. This is good, and it is pleasing in the sight of God our Savior" (1 Timothy 2:1-3). These verses are loaded with application. In three short verses we learn that God wants us praying for our leaders, that our prayers are effective, that praying helps us live "peaceful and quiet" lives, and most importantly, that praying for our leaders pleases "God our Savior."

Fifth, study your local voters' guide so you are fully informed on the issues and the candidates. It's easy to vote a straight ticket, but it may not be the best option. It takes a little extra effort, but it's wise to grab a voters' guide in order to cast a more informed vote.

Last, remember joyfully that there's coming a day when Jesus will set up His kingdom and there will be no more need to vote (see Revelation 21:1-5). The next time we think about voting for an earthly ruler, let us not forget that it is far more important who will rule our hearts than who is going to rule the United States. Our greatest honor as Christians is to campaign for Jesus by calling a lost and broken world to a gracious and healing Savior.

■ Thought to Ponder
Before we vote we need to be more than just inspired. We need to be informed.

■ Memory Verse
Choose for your tribes wise, understanding, and experienced men, and I will appoint them as your heads (Deuteronomy 1:13).

■ Question to Consider
If someone is clueless about the candidates they're voting for, should they still vote?

■ One-Minute Apologist Video
https://www.youtube.com/watch?v=1dGjLHV1CKE

Does God Approve of Homosexual Behavior?

> *Having a legitimate need for intimacy cannot justify illegitimate ways of fulfilling that need...If the only thing that really turns me on sexually and emotionally is Activity B, yet only Activity A is sanctioned by God, then I cannot rewrite the rules to accommodate my taste.*
>
> JOE DALLAS

Homosexuality is no longer an "in the closet" issue. The closet door has swung wide open and the door is completely off the hinges. We are living in the midst of a moral revolution, a revolution accelerating at speeds so fast that it's hard to even process.

This topic deserves more detail than I can provide in this book, and writing about it in such brief fashion feels almost trite. The last thing I want to do is sound bigoted, hurtful, or insensitive. Neither do I want to compromise my conscience or dilute Scripture in the name of cultural appeasement or political correctness. Therefore, with these limitations in mind, here are a few thoughts.

First, just because we disagree with someone doesn't necessarily *make us a bigot.* There are plenty of bigots in the world. There are Christians who are bigoted toward homosexuals and there are homosexuals who are bigoted toward Christians. And guess what? There are Christians and homosexuals who disagree with each other's worldview, but they truly respect and like each other on a personal level. And that's encouraging. The homosexuals that I have known have been very respectful to me, and I believe they would say the same thing about my attitude toward them. Fortunately, it's possible to discuss homosexuality without insisting, "Agree with me or you're a bigot." The good news is we can disagree and befriend one another.

Second, to use the Bible to teach same-sex marriage is to be guilty of eisegesis. Eisegesis commits the fallacy of reading *into* the text what we want it to say versus extracting *out* of the text what it actually says, which is exegesis. As scriptural interpreters, our job is to get at the authors' intended meaning and to resist the temptation to bend the Scriptures to fit our desires.

As hard as it may be to come to terms with, the Bible is clear regarding its teaching that homosexual behavior is not God's plan (Genesis 19; Leviticus 18:22; Romans 1:26-27; 1 Corinthians 6:9-10). Yet, in an attempt to satisfy their own desires or to appease the culture, many would-be interpreters seek to make the Bible say otherwise. This kind of eisegesis must be avoided. At all costs.

Third, read a few of the more recent resources to sharpen your understanding of what the Scripture teaches regarding homosexuality. I realize I'm leaving a lot of unanswered questions in this simple reply, so here are three books that I recommend for further study.

- *What Does the Bible Really Teach About Homosexuality?* by Kevin DeYoung
- *Same-Sex Marriage* by Sean McDowell and John Stonestreet
- *The Secret Thoughts of an Unlikely Convert* by Rosaria Butterfield

If there's ever been a time for hardcore discernment, that time is now. This moral revolution is moving with such rapidity that we have become easy targets for self-deception. This means we must really know our stuff lest we too become deceived. The great ancient orator Demosthenes once quipped, "Nothing is so easy as to deceive oneself; for what we wish, we readily believe."

Now, that's a warning for all of us.

■ Thought to Ponder
Our sexuality is not our identity.

■ Memory Verse
You shall not lie with a male as with a woman; it is an abomination (Leviticus 18:22).

■ Question to Consider
How can we move from being so either/or as a culture and make relational progress despite our differences of opinion or conviction?

■ One-Minute Apologist Video
Bobby Conway, "How Can the Church Engage the Homosexual Community?"
www.youtube.com/watch?v=LOdUCgZkvsI

Did Love Win in the Supreme Court Ruling on Same-Sex Marriage?

> *I don't doubt that for most same-sex couples the longing for marriage is sincere, heartfelt, and without a desire to harm anyone else's marriage. And yet, same-sex unions cannot be accepted as marriage without devaluing all marriages, because the only way to embrace same-sex partnerships as marriage is by changing what marriage means altogether.*
>
> KEVIN DEYOUNG

On Friday morning, June 26, 2015, my wife and I were sitting on the couch when a breaking news report interrupted our program to inform us that in a 5-4 decision, the Supreme Court had ruled same-sex marriage legal in all fifty states. Undoubtedly, this decision will become one of the most monumental court decisions ever made on American soil.

Shortly after the news report, President Obama's Twitter feed said, "Today is a big step in our march toward equality. Gay and lesbian couples now have the right to marry, just like anyone else. LoveWins." I said to my wife, "What I've always loved about being a Christian is its generous extension of love to all peoples. But now, love has been redefined in such a way that if we don't change our moral posture, we won't be considered loving after all."

Yet, isn't it possible to be compassionate without compromise? Can't we accept each other without agreeing with each other? Isn't there room to respect each other's conscience?

Apparently not. The new anthem is "Agree or else..." And what about the dissenters—the Christians, Jews, Muslims, and many others who disagree with the vote? Will they not be loved until they agree? Will love win for them?

It now appears that love wins only if you approve of homosexuality. That saddens me.

In the end, real love isn't agreeing with everyone, nor is it approving of everything somebody does. Real love is loving people in spite of our disagreements. And that's what makes Christianity so special, so unique, and so beautiful. It's the kind of love Jesus modeled when He spent time with sinners who lived lifestyles He didn't agree with. At the same time, He did not bend His values to make them feel accepted. Rather, Jesus had a wonderful way of making many He didn't agree with feel accepted and loved.

So what are we to do as Christians? I'll tell you. Love the homosexual. Love the Muslim. Love the Hindu. Love the Buddhist and the transgender and the hipster and the polygamist and the drug addict and the prostitute. But by all means, let's not adopt their views to prove our love. Let's love those we don't agree with. That's when love *really* wins.

▥ Thought to Ponder

The moment the gospel is gutted of truth or love it ceases to be the bona fide gospel.

Memory Verse

Rather, speaking the truth in love, we are to grow up in every way into him who is the head, into Christ (Ephesians 4:15).

Question to Consider

What are some ways a Christian can show compassion without compromise as it relates to same-sex marriage?

One-Minute Apologist Video

Bobby Conway, "Did Love Win with the Supreme Court Ruling?"

www.youtube.com/watch?v=N3757HGFJ3k

Does the Bible Approve of Polygamy?

> *It's not unusual to hear critics say, based on certain Old Testament texts, that God actually endorses polygamy/bigamy. However, if God commended or commanded such a practice, this would be a deviation from the assumed standard of heterosexual monogamy in Genesis 2:24 and elsewhere.*
>
> PAUL COPAN

While the Bible acknowledges polygamy, it doesn't approve of it. Every seminary student worth his salt knows that the Bible doesn't approve of everything it records. That's Bible 101. The Bible discusses lots of things that is doesn't permit. And frankly, I'm thankful for that. The Bible is a transparent book. Rather than covering up the sins of those who lived before us, it records them so that we can learn from our spiritual predecessors.

From the very first book of the Bible, God's plan for monogamous marriage is laid out, "A man shall leave his father and his mother and hold fast to his wife, and they shall become one flesh" (Genesis 2:24). Adding to this, the Bible warns Israel's kings not to take multiple wives (Deuteronomy 17:17). Furthermore, in the New Testament, we read that church leaders must be "the husband of *one* wife" (1 Timothy 3:2). Kings and church leaders were to set the moral temperature for their communities. What was expected of them was certainly desired for their community.

Not surprisingly, many of the leaders failed to uphold God's standard for monogamous marriage. And the fact that God still graciously blessed Abraham, Jacob, David, Solomon, and others in spite of their polygamous relationships doesn't mean He condoned their actions. It just means that God works with what He's got and that's because He's a gracious and merciful God.

It's a relief to know that God doesn't allow our sin or the sin of our forefathers to thwart His overall redemptive plan. Regardless of our actions, God's plans will still prevail.

Thought to Ponder
God often works through us in spite of us. And that's comforting.

Memory Verse
And he shall not acquire many wives for himself, lest his heart turn away, nor shall he acquire for himself excessive silver and gold (Deuteronomy 17:17).

Question to Consider
Why does God place a premium on monogamous marriage?

One-Minute Apologist Video
Bobby Conway, "Does the Bible Approve Polygamy?"
www.youtube.com/watch?v=bijJkIQzes4

Can Tolerance Be a Good Thing?

The correct basis of tolerance is not relativism, but love.

WILLIAM LANE CRAIG

Tolerance can be positive and negative. Traditionally, tolerance was seen as a virtue where opposing ideologies were allowed to compete at the table of ideas. Great value was placed on accepting people even though you disagreed with them. But today, tolerance has been imbedded with new meaning: "If you disagree with me, you're a bigot." If there was ever a sordid view of tolerance, that's it.

In today's western world, tolerance now means that we need to accept all truth claims as equally valid in order to show acceptance. This form of tolerance is not only twisted, it's self-refuting. The very idea of tolerance means that you *don't agree* with the other person's viewpoint, but in the name of love and respect for humanity, you accept that person's right to embrace another view. It's quite possible to accept each other without agreeing with each other. That takes love, grace, growth, understanding, and the right kind of tolerance.

Unfortunately, today's "tolerance" stifles free speech, even working against the First Amendment. Who wants to *truly* speak their mind if it means being branded a bigot? The good kind of tolerance welcomes free speech and opposing views, knowing that this will bear fruit in honest exchange. Besides, it's too much to insist that we all agree with each other before we can accept one another. Jesus modeled this beautifully. Sinners loved being around Him because He had a way of accepting people He disagreed with. Jesus tolerated others without tailoring His own views. That's the negative side of tolerance—when one starts bending their beliefs in the name of tolerance.

Let's avoid that.

■ Thought to Ponder
Tolerance doesn't mean tailoring the truth to make your views more palatable to others. It means loving others even when they won't tailor their views for you.

■ Memory Verse
I therefore, a prisoner for the Lord, urge you to walk in a manner worthy of the calling to which you have been called, with all humility and gentleness, with patience, bearing with one another in love (Ephesians 4:1-2).

■ Question to Consider
Where do you see this negative side of tolerance played out in today's culture?

■ One-Minute Apologist Video
Bobby Conway, "Can Tolerance Be a Good Thing?"
www.youtube.com/watch?v=h_Uoi3-ggHo

Are Christians Narrow-Minded?

It is not narrow-minded if you've looked into it and found that Christianity proves itself trustworthy in ways that other religions and viewpoints do not.

PAUL COPAN

You Christians are so narrow-minded." Sound familiar? I'm sure it does. And who wants to be thought of in such gloomy terms? I'd like to think of myself as broadminded, reasonable, willing to hear the opinions of others, thoughtful and considerate. And I'm guessing you would too. So, how can we answer the objection that Christians are narrow-minded?

First, ask the other person what they mean by "narrow-minded." This will unearth a lot and help focus the conversation. And it'll also provide an opportunity to apologize for a possible wrong committed by the church or even to concede a valid point. But be prepared to admit that Christians are narrow-minded if believing that Jesus is the only way to heaven is being narrow-minded. Those aren't my words. They originated with Jesus Himself. He said, "I am the way, and the truth, and the life. No one comes to the Father except through me" (John 14:6). The way to heaven is exclusive—through Jesus. Heaven is a universal offer through an exclusive person—Jesus Christ. Therefore, I admit I'm narrow-minded about who can save me, but I'm wide-minded about who can be saved.

Second, demonstrate how everyone is narrow-minded. For example, Muslims believe Allah is the only true God, and if you disagree, they will say you're wrong. But isn't that equally narrow-minded? Or what about the relativist? They believe truth is relative, but if you disagree and say that truth is absolute, they'll fault you. Isn't that narrow-minded? Atheists believe there is no God, and if you believe in God, they will say you are wrong. Isn't that narrow-minded? Polytheists believe there are many gods, but if you believe in only one God or reject all gods, they'll say you're wrong. Isn't that narrow-minded?

Or consider one final example—surely the religious pluralists, who believe all roads lead to heaven, can't be narrow-minded. But not so fast. They too find themselves in the same predicament. They believe there are many ways to heaven, but if you believe there is only one way to heaven or no way to heaven, they will say that you're wrong. Isn't that narrow-minded too?

Of course.

Everyone is narrow-minded. Even the view that says there is no such thing as right believes they are right about their claim that there is no such thing as right. Even the person who thinks you can't know what truth is believes it's true that you can't know what truth is. Make sense?

Truth by its very nature has a narrow feature to it. For example, 6 x 6 = 36. There are no married bachelors. Neither is there such a thing as square circles. Are you narrow-minded to believe that? Of course not. It is what it is. And let's be honest. Don't we all want a little narrow-mindedness from time to time? When I visit the doctor, I want him to be narrow-minded about the treatment he recommends for my condition. I don't want him to think he can prescribe whatever he *feels* like. I want him to give me what he believes to be right. I also want the driver on the opposite side of the road to remain narrow-minded about staying in his lane. I don't want him to broaden his path. If he does, we both may die.

So the next time someone accuses you of being narrow-minded, remind him in a gracious way that you are not alone. While I don't like the term *narrow-minded* and don't want to be considered narrow-minded in the pejorative sense, I'm thankful there's an easy explanation for the often repeated claim that Christians are narrow-minded.

■ Thought to Ponder

Being narrow-minded isn't an exclusively Christian issue—it's a human issue.

■ Memory Verse

And there is salvation in no one else, for there is no other name under heaven given among men by which we must be saved (Acts 4:12).

■ Question to Consider

When people accuse Christians of being narrow-minded, what do you think they're really getting at? Is there anything we can learn from this type of criticism?

■ One-Minute Apologist Video

Bobby Conway, "Are Christians Narrow-Minded?"
www.youtube.com/watch?v=YUY15hfPrDM

Is the Future Hopeless for Today's Youth?

We cannot always build the future for our youth, but we can build our youth for the future.

FRANKLIN D. ROOSEVELT

It's no secret that today's youth have their work cut out for them. And so do the parents, teachers, coaches, student pastors, and other adult influencers of these kids. All of these leaders must dig extra deep to offer a generous dose of Christian hope.

If today's youth continue to hear, "I'd hate to be you" or "I can't imagine living in your shoes," they may grow weary. They may even think, *So my situation looks hopeless to you?* Think about it. Is it possible that we are unintentionally creating despair in our youth? Is our pessimism adding to their hopelessness? If so, isn't it time we change our tone a bit? Is there not hope, Christian? Or have we built our confidence on the quicksand of the "American Dream"? If so, get ready to be disillusioned, if you aren't already.

To make matters worse, the church at large is in a tenuous state, and these kids are waffling with doubts. Many Christian teens who really want to live for Christ muse about their future and think, *So, it's possible that I'll inherit trillions of dollars of debt, I won't be able to land a job after college, I'm may get persecuted for my faith, and chances are my marriage won't last. And oh, to top it off, I'm constantly being told by skeptics that my faith is a joke. Some life.*

Both families and churches need to get in touch with what these kids are feeling and use what they reveal to build out an equipping strategy of hope. Our kids need to know the darker it gets, the more their light can shine. Like Esther, they need to know that they've been created for such a time as this (Esther 4:14). They need to know that every obstacle is an opportunity to lead large. And by all means, they need to know that the Christian adults in their lives are ready to lead the way, hope style.

■ Thought to Ponder

No matter how hopeless our culture gets, the gospel always promises a hopeful future.

■ Memory Verse

Train up a child in the way he should go; even when he is old he will not depart from it (Proverbs 22:6).

■ Question to Consider

What are some ways that you can be a voice of hope for today's youth?

■ One-Minute Apologist Video

Bobby Conway, "Is the Future Hopeless for Today's Youth?" www.youtube.com/watch?v=DzOCButUVuI

What Is Sin?

Certain new theologians dispute original sin, which is the only part of Christian theology which can really be proved.

G.K. CHESTERTON

Sin is not a popular word. And I can see why. Who enjoys thinking of himself as a sinner? Even those who don't know what the word means know it has a negative connotation. But what exactly is sin?

Biblically, to sin means to fall short of God's standard of righteousness. Paul said it like this: "All have sinned and fall short of the glory of God" (Romans 3:23). The moral chasm between God and man is so wide that it devastates *all* of us. No one can meet this standard. Sin affects us all.

How has humanity sought to deal with the systemic problem of sin?

First, this moral dilemma has caused some people to try to reach the standard on their own. But if there was ever a vain pursuit, this is it. I'm all for someone striving to live righteously, but not if that person thinks they can obtain moral perfection on their own. Impossible.

Second, some people seek to minimize God's standards in order to feel better about themselves. They do this by reducing God's demands in order to reach them. Others may even proclaim themselves as the standard and thereby strive to feel good about themselves by finding someone who appears worse off, more twisted. But that does nothing to remove the *real* standard. It only allows one to live self-deceived, thinking they're truly righteous. God's standard doesn't shrink. It's nonadjustable.

Third, others seek to remove the standard altogether. As Fyodor Dostoyevsky once said, "If God does not exist, everything is permissible." There is no such thing as sin without the standard. And if there is no sin, then there is no guilt, and if there is no guilt, then by all means eat, drink, and be merry, right? Wrong. There is guilt because there is sin, and there is sin because there is a standard, and there is a standard because there is a God. God is the standard.

I remember on one occasion reflecting on this standard with discouragement. I thought, *God, this doesn't seem right. We are held accountable for not meeting an impossible standard. We are basically judged for not being as righteous as You. And to be so we'd have to be You—we'd have to be God, but we're not.* I further thought to myself, *That'd be like me taking my son to New York City and leaving him on the street while I went to the top of the Empire State Building, placed a basketball rim over the side of the building, and yelled to him from the top floor, "All right, Dawson, let me see you slam-dunk this."* Can you imagine how silly he'd look down on the street trying to slam-dunk a basketball into a rim that is 102 floors high? It'd be futile. And it'd look absurd. Worse yet, imagine me punishing him for not meeting this impossible standard that I set up.

In a similar way, we all fall silly short of achieving God's moral standard. But God doesn't expect us to keep the standard, *unless* we're planning on getting to heaven apart from Jesus. And that's not happening. Not for me or anyone else. God knows that we can't keep the standard. So He pulled off the ultimate slam dunk for us by sending Jesus to meet the standard on our behalf. Now all we need to do is believe that Jesus substituted Himself for us by dying on the cross in order to pay for our sins. Now we can be counted as righteous by faith. That's some good news right there.

It turns out that we're not judged for failing to meet the standard.

We are judged for what we do with Jesus.

■ Thought to Ponder
God is a sin-forgiving God.

■ Memory Verse
None is righteous, no, not one (Romans 3:10).

■ Question to Consider
It doesn't take a genius to realize that *sin* isn't a popular word these days. Why are some people so put off by that word?

■ One-Minute Apologist Video
Hank Hanegraaff, "What Is Sin?"
www.youtube.com/watch?v=ut0StLJU4jk

Is Abortion a Sin?

> *Prolife advocates don't oppose abortion because they find it distasteful; they oppose it because it violates rational moral principles. The negative emotional response follows from the moral wrongness of the act.*
>
> SCOTT KLUSENDORF

The greatest war in our culture today is taking place in the womb—*the war on the womb*. More casualties have occurred in the womb than in any other location in human history. Since *Roe v. Wade* was passed in 1973, there have been approximately fifty-five million abortions in America alone. That's staggering. And the greater tragedy is this war is far from over. Sadly, abortion continues to be a cultural hot button, which means we continue to need voices for the voiceless.

Some might say, "But why? Isn't abortion legal in America?" Yes, but *legal doesn't equal legit*. Just because something is declared right doesn't make it right. Others maintain that abortion is necessary in certain circumstances for the mother's health or in the event of rape. But well-known statistics show that rape cases make up only 1 percent of all abortions and a woman's health is a deciding factor only 3 percent of the time. This means roughly 96 percent of all abortions take place because the mother or father is often unwilling to take the responsibility to parent the child or to put the child up for adoption. This must change, but how?

First, we need to realize that human beings are created in God's image (Genesis 1:26-27). Scott Klusendorf, the founder and president of Life Training Institute (http://prolifetraining.com), has developed the acronym SLED to demonstrate the similarities between a newborn and a preborn. SLED stands for size, level of development, environment (the location of the child), and degree of dependency. Each letter is meant to show how a preborn is just as human as a newborn.

Even if a person denies that we are created by God or in His image, if they honestly face the facts, they cannot maintain that the child within the womb isn't a human being. That position is intellectually dishonest. Scott's argument is effective because one can use it without even bringing the Bible into play with those not interested in hearing what the Scriptures have to say.

Second, abortion is wrong because it breaks the sixth commandment. The Bible says, "You shall not murder" (Exodus 20:13). Amazingly, in our culture, if a person murders a pregnant woman, he can be tried for double murder, but if the mother aborts her child, she walks free and is even celebrated as courageous by some. Yet, many women *and* men who have experienced the hurt of choosing abortion over life don't truly walk free. They experience emotional, spiritual, and physical problems due to the trauma caused from having an abortion.

Third, God knit us together in the womb. Look at these verses from Psalm 139:13-16 and let them sink in,

> For you formed my inward parts;
>   you knitted me together in my mother's womb.
> I praise you, for I am fearfully and wonderfully made.
> Wonderful are your works;
>   my soul knows it very well.
> My frame was not hidden from you,

> when I was being made in secret,
>   intricately woven in the depths of the earth.
> Your eyes saw my unformed substance;
> in your book were written, every one of them,
>   the days that were formed for me,
>   when as yet there was none of them.

Think about it. Abortion aborts the process described in these verses from taking place.

I realize this is a hard issue for those who have had abortions and are now living with the guilt of their decision. While guilt is the proper emotion for violating God's moral law, grace is God's response to those who acknowledge their wrongs. Let me encourage you to turn to God and ask for forgiveness, and then trust that He'll readily forgive (1 John 1:9).

Now that's comforting.

■ Thought to Ponder

Abortion is the holocaust of our time.

■ Memory Verse

Before I formed you in the womb I knew you, and before you were born I consecrated you; I appointed you a prophet to the nations (Jeremiah 1:5).

■ Question to Consider

What are some ways that you and your church can be a voice for the voiceless?

■ One-Minute Apologist Video

Mark Mittelberg, "What Should Be the Church's Tone on Abortion?"
www.youtube.com/watch?v=uOVELBD6pyU

Is God a Genocidal Maniac?

At the conquest, God poured out his judgment on a wicked society who deserved it; at the cross, God bore on himself the judgment of God on human wickedness, through the person of his own sinless Son—who deserved it not one bit.

CHRISTOPHER WRIGHT

The New Atheists love to paint God as a genocidal maniac. Many critics of the Bible have accused Christians of serving a maniacal God who obliterates many seemingly innocent nations in the Old Testament. At first blush it may seem as if God is a moral tyrant, but this is not the case. Look at it this way.

First, no one is truly innocent. Paul helps us here: "All have sinned and fall short of the glory of God" (Romans 3:23). In the same letter, Paul teaches us that everyone is without excuse before God (Romans 1:20). This means that a person doesn't have to be a Christian in order to know right from wrong. We come programmed with an innate sense of moral values. And that's because God's moral code is built-in. The Scriptures teach us that both conscience and creation testify to God's there-ness and greatness (Romans 1:19-20; Psalm 19:1; Romans 2:14-16).

Second, judgment is God's last resort. Aren't you grateful? I sure am. God patiently waited 430 years to judge the inhabitants of Canaan because their sin had not reached its limit (Genesis 15:16).

With Sodom and Gomorrah, Abraham successfully pleaded for them, asking God to spare them for the sake of ten righteous people (Genesis 18–19). Genesis 6:3 may indicate that Noah warned of coming judgment for 120 years before God actually judged the earth with a flood (see also 2 Peter 2:5). Even the not-so-popular Old Testament prophets who warned of impending judgment depict God's mercy by giving rebel nations a heads-up to repent. God readily showed mercy to those willing to turn from sin as seen with Nineveh (Jonah 3) and Rahab right before the conquest (Joshua 2). God doesn't judge out of the blue. He graciously warns before He judges.

Third, God's destruction was never the result of ethnic cleansing; rather, it was to cleanse idolatry, as in the case of the Canaanite conquest. Even the Israelites went into captivity in part because of their idolatry, and God used both the Assyrians and the Babylonians to chasten them for their continuous rebellion in order to turn their hearts back to Him.

Know this. Judgment isn't God's first resort. It's His last resort. Far from being a genocidal maniac, God even took our judgment upon Himself in order to spare us His judgment. Think Jesus. Think the cross. Think grace.

▦ Thought to Ponder

The reason we struggle so much with God's judgment is because we fail to realize the great chasm between God's holiness and mankind's sinfulness.

Memory Verse

Far be it from you to do such a thing, to put the righteous to death with the wicked, so that the righteous fare as the wicked! Far be that from you! Shall not the Judge of all the earth do what is just? (Genesis 18:25).

Question to Consider

Why are we so quick to focus on God's judgments versus our sinfulness?

One-Minute Apologist Video

Bobby Conway, "How Can a Loving God Kill People in the Old Testament?" www.youtube.com/watch?v=zvV3l_dVvFc

How Does Evil Reveal the Greatness of God?

> *When we cannot trace God's hand, we must simply trust his heart.*
>
> CHARLES SPURGEON

You've probably heard the statement, "If God is good, why is there evil?" But here is a twist: "Can evil demonstrate something beautiful about the greatness of God?"

It can. While many can picture a nirvana free from the stain of sin, few can digest a good, loving God who has allowed our world to be permeated with evil. While a world tarnished by sin exposes our depravity, with God it provides a greater opportunity for certain attributes of His to be revealed that otherwise would have remained concealed. For example, because we live in a fallen world, we are able to experience God in a way that would be impossible had the Fall never occurred.

As evil as the Fall was, it has afforded us the opportunity to experience God's grace, mercy, forgiveness, and unconditional love. Those attributes of God are highlighted against our sin. Without sin, what need is there for grace, mercy, and forgiveness? If sin had never entered the world, how would we *really* know that we are loved *un*conditionally? Perhaps we were loved because of our perfections. But God's love is deeper, richer, and more stunning as it is highlighted against the backdrop of our depravity.

The greatness of God was revealed most splendidly at the cross where Jesus Christ looked into the evil face of our sin and demonstrated through His death that we are loved unconditionally by a gracious, merciful, and forgiving God we call Yahweh.

■ Thought to Ponder

God is so good that even when evil enters the picture, hidden aspects of His greatness crystalize before thinking minds.

■ Memory Verse

O Lord, our Lord, how majestic is your name in all the earth! You have set your glory above the heavens (Psalm 8:1).

■ Question to Consider

How can thinking about these aspects of God now revealed in our fallen world help you appreciate God's greatness?

■ One-Minute Apologist Video

Bobby Conway, "How Can Evil Reveal God's Greatness?" www.youtube.com/watch?v=xvUFzzsM5ts

If God Is Good, Why Is There Evil?

There is an old illusion. It is called good and evil.

FRIEDRICH NIETZSCHE

Perhaps the most frequently asked *why* question is, "If God is good, *why* is there evil?" This question is so jarring that many cannot stomach the idea of a God who could allow for the ghastly, unspeakable evil we see in our world. Is it possible for a good God to exist in the presence of such malevolence? I mean, seriously, can there really be a *good* God?

Atheists don't think so. And their argument goes something like this: If God is omnipotent (all-powerful), He can get rid of evil. And if God is omnibenevolent (all-good), He will get rid of evil. Yet, evil still exists. Therefore, God does not exist.

Sound familiar? For the atheist, this argument solves the problem, eliminating two problems: the problem of evil *and* the problem of God. But not so fast. There's another problem. The problem is, this argument is invalid.

Let's look a little closer.

While it is true that God is all-powerful and all-good and that evil exists, it doesn't necessarily follow that God doesn't exist simply because evil exists. God and the presence of evil *both* exist. Before we deal directly with the argument against God's existence, let me first mention a few qualifications about evil.

First, evil isn't a thing in itself. It's more like an adjective than a noun. There are evil leaders and evil motives and evil wars and evil thoughts. Second, philosophers also distinguish between moral and natural evils. Moral evils are things like murder, rape, adultery, and stealing, whereas natural evils are tornadoes, tsunamis, earthquakes, and the like. Third, some philosophers distinguish between the emotional problem of evil and the intellectual problem of evil. This is helpful. The presence of evil affects us emotionally, and it's hard to get around it. We've all felt its effects. But this angst that we feel, as disturbing as it is, doesn't pose an intellectual problem for God's existence. That's because there is no contradiction in contending that both evil and God exist.

With this is mind, the argument before us implodes. It fallaciously *assumes* that an omnipotent and omnibenevolent God couldn't have any *good reasons* for allowing such rampant evil in the world. But how could we possibly know God's mind on such things? There's a massive assumption that we know what is best in stating that God would not allow evil. And while it may be hard to wrap our heads around the evil that is so prevalent, we can know that God has His purposes beyond our ability to see.

▇ Thought to Ponder

Thankfully our questions about the exhaustive purposes of evil can be entrusted to a God who cares.

▇ Memory Verse

Though the fig tree should not blossom,
    nor fruit be on the vines,
the produce of the olive fail
    and the fields yield no food,
the flock be cut off from the fold
    and there be no herd in the stalls,

> yet I will rejoice in the LORD;
>   I will take joy in the God of my salvation.
>   (Habakkuk 3:17-18)

▓ Question to Consider

Can you think of any biblical examples (or other examples for that matter) whereby God brought good out of evil and it turned out to serve a meaningful purpose?

▓ One-Minute Apologist Video

Brett Kunkle, "Why Does God Allow Suffering and Evil?"
www.youtube.com/watch?v=5gcL157SlPA

Why Did God Allow Stoning?

> *Most capital sanctions functioned as a kind of rhetorical denunciation which expressed, in vivid form, a moral ideal. Further, in practice, a ransom was paid and the punishment was not literally carried out.*
>
> MATTHEW FLANNAGAN

Certain portions of Scripture are harder to grasp than others. Such is the case with the stoning passages (see Leviticus 20:27; 24:16; Numbers 15:32-36; Deuteronomy 13:6-11; 21:18-21). I can understand capital punishment, but stoning just seems so barbaric, cruel, and harsh, especially when the commandment is issued to parents to indict rebellious sons, as seen in Deuteronomy 21:18-21:

> If a man has a stubborn and rebellious son who will not obey the voice of his father or the voice of his mother, and, though they discipline him, will not listen to them, then his father and his mother shall take hold of him and bring him out to the elders of his city at the gate of the place where he lives, and they shall say to the elders of his city, "This our son is stubborn and rebellious; he will not obey our voice; he is a glutton and a drunkard." Then all the men of the city shall

> stone him to death with stones. So you shall purge the
> evil from your midst, and all Israel shall hear, and fear.

This is a hard passage to stomach, don't you think? I prefer death by lethal injection, but stoning? What a mess. As believers, how are we to understand these verses?

First, we need to understand this text, like all texts, in context. We can't overlay our twenty-first century cultural understanding on this ancient milieu. Nothing will lead to more head-scratching confusion and frustration than that. Ours is a culture where a little swat causes a big sweat. No wonder stoning is extra hard for us to digest.

Second, stoning was the last resort. The son described in these verses exhibits an unbending and rebellious spirit. He's steeped in sin, freely giving himself to drunkenness and gluttony, and refuses to respond to any parental discipline, altogether shunning the fifth commandment. These verses describe a seemingly hopeless case, one set in his own ways as he strong-arms God, his parents, and the principles of his surrounding theocratic nation. He's a leper-like son whose sin will spread and undo the moral fabric of his nation if left unchecked. Once the parents realize their son's recalcitrance, they seek outside intervention as a final resort.

Third, the ultimate purpose of stoning was to purge evil from the community and to create a healthy fear of living an unchecked moral life. The health of the nation depended on the entire community walking in step with God. That's not to say people didn't sin. They did. A lot. And there was an entire sacrificial system in place so people could once again obtain a clear conscience before the Lord. The son described in these verses wasn't looking for a clear conscience—his conscience was seared.

Fourth, this wasn't a common custom. Interestingly enough, we have very few instances of stoning that take place in the biblical records and I'm not aware of any extra-biblical evidence that this punishment was commonly carried out. Perhaps the threat was enough to deter people from such rebellious behavior.

Finally, Jesus models the heart of God regarding stoning. In John 8:7 Jesus said to those who accused the adulterous woman, "Let him who is without sin among you be the first to throw a stone at her."* The law teaches us that we are all lawbreakers. Everyone under God's law deserves capital punishment, but Jesus experienced capital punishment on our behalf even though He was the only one to ever fulfill the law. Essentially, He was stoned for us in an act of unconditional love as He experienced death on our behalf.

▨ Thought to Ponder
We should be honest enough to admit that there's no getting around the fact that some passages of Scripture are harder to understand or relate to than others.

▨ Memory Verse
Have I any pleasure in the death of the wicked, declares the Lord GOD, and not rather that he should turn from his way and live? (Ezekiel 18:23).

▨ Question to Consider
Do you feel prepared to field questions from people regarding the difficult topic of stoning?

▨ One-Minute Apologist Video
Bobby Conway, "Why Did God Allow Stoning?"
https://www.youtube.com/watch?v=S95V6H9lwQw

---

* I realize our earliest manuscripts do not include John 7:53–8:11. Regardless, these verses depict a consistent vision of the life and actions of Jesus Christ.

Is God an Angry God?

*Although believers by nature are far from God,
and children of wrath, even as others, yet it is
amazing to think how nigh they are brought
to him again by the blood of Jesus Christ.*

GEORGE WHITEFIELD

Is God fuming at the world? A sort of enraged deity who's foaming at the mouth because of the sins of mankind? To answer this question fairly, we must first qualify what we mean by God's anger.

It doesn't take long when reading the Bible to see that the Scriptures teach that God is perfectly holy and *sinless.* The Bible also says, "Be angry and do not sin" (Ephesians 4:26). Though this verse is an admonition to humans, it nevertheless shows us that it's possible to be angry and *not* sin.

With these thoughts before us, we are now ready to answer our question, "Is God an angry God?" Well, this may shock you, but I hope so.

Before you react, remember we are talking about sinless anger. An anger that's controlled, justified, warranted, and perfectly holy. We are *not* talking about some out-of-control, flying-off-the-handle, teenage-temper-tantrum anger. And we must refrain from drawing a direct association between our human anger and God's anger. He's in a league of His own. However, with a little reflection, we can see that God's anger is not only justifiable, it's understandable.

Do we really want to serve and love a God who doesn't get angry? Aren't there some things worth getting a little fired up about? Picture a passive God who is totally detached and uninterested in human affairs, a God who reasons to Himself, "Rape? Oh, what's the big deal? Pedophilia? People just need to lighten up. Murder? Chill out already." Suppose your spouse was raped or murdered? Would you still feel good about an anger-free God? Of course not. Who wants to serve a dispassionate, indifferent, apathetic God?

Some might contend, "Of course we want God to be enraged by rape, pedophilia, and murder, but those are extreme examples." Are they? And if so, aren't we now falling into the trap of creating a God of our own making and determining what He can and cannot be angry at? That's where it gets subjective. We don't make the laws. God does. The Bible is not a buffet whereby one picks and chooses what he likes and discards what he doesn't.

Deep down, any healthy and sane person wants justice to be meted out on the evils they've observed or even experienced firsthand. We just don't want it meted out on us. We'd rather experience some good old-fashioned grace. At least I would. And I trust I'm not alone.

God is a just God. And He has a right to be angry. As we've discussed, there's both righteous anger and unrighteous anger. But God *always* models righteous anger. His anger is rooted in His love. He loves the world so much that it angers Him when we self-destruct and miss out on maximizing our life.

Thankfully for us, His anger, His holy and justifiable wrath, was poured out on Christ on the cross so that whoever believes in Him can encounter—not an angry, grieved, brokenhearted God, but a gracious, loving, and compassionate Savior.

■ Thought to Ponder

In the absence of righteous anger is a lack of holy love.

■ Memory Verse

The wrath of God is revealed from heaven against all ungodliness and unrighteousness of men, who by their unrighteousness suppress the truth (Romans 1:18).

■ Question to Consider

What biblical examples of God's righteous anger can you think of? What type of consequences might a church encounter if it refuses to talk about the wrath of God?

■ One-Minute Apologist Video

Bobby Conway, "Is God an Angry God?"
www.youtube.com/watch?v=cnFrdLwhCkc

Is the God of the Old Testament the Same God of the New Testament?

> *The God that Jesus worshipped and proclaimed is the God of the Old Testament.*
>
> WILLIAM LANE CRAIG

Many people wrongly assume that the God of the New Testament differs from the God of the Old Testament. They do so because they perceive the God of the Old Testament as a moody and volatile curmudgeon, while perceiving the God of the New Testament as a judge-free, grace-giving, glorified sugar daddy. So does the Bible present a clash of the Gods? The omnibenevolent God of the New Testament versus the omnimalevolent God of the Old Testament?

The short answer is no. While I can see how people arrive at such a conclusion with a simple glance at Scripture, I cannot see how the claim holds sway with a steady gaze. For the neophyte Bible student, *possibly*, but for the honest Bible scholar, *implausible*. Even a fresh devotee can see a consistent portrait of the one true God.

Upon closer inspection of Scripture, it is clear that God is gracious and just and that both of these qualities are depicted in *both* the Old and the New Testaments. I'll concede that one sees the evidence of God's grace perhaps more distinctly in the New Testament, where His grace is spiked home at the cross through Jesus's atoning death, but that doesn't mean that the God of the Old Testament was devoid of grace.

Not at all.

Let's consider a tad of the ample evidence. From the very first book of the Bible, God's grace was swiftly applied in order to cover the first human sin (Genesis 3:21). Furthermore, as we work our way through the Old Testament, God's grace continues to emerge. For example, take the prophets. These so-called "messengers of judgment" were also "messengers of mercy." Think about it. God didn't owe those in outright rebellion against Him a warning. A siren. A wakeup call. The very fact that they were warned over and over again is a sure symbol of God's love and willingness to shower His people with grace.

And His grace isn't restrictive either. No, it's without borders. His grace has tentacles reaching wide and far. Consider the Ninevites. The prophet Jonah knew full well that God is gracious, so much so that he resented it. He even ran from God in an attempt to avoid being God's messenger. Following God's downpour of mercy and grace on the Ninevites, Jonah prayed, "O LORD, is not this what I said when I was yet in my country? That is why I made haste to flee to Tarshish; for I knew that you are a gracious God and merciful, slow to anger and abounding in steadfast love, and relenting from disaster" (Jonah 4:2).

Just as God's unconditional grace is seen in the Old Testament, so too, His holy justice is ubiquitous in the New Testament. Try reading Romans 1–3 and then saying, "God's not just." Or consider the story of Jesus clearing the temple (Mark 11:15-17). There you see God's righteous wrath *in the flesh*. Furthermore, consider how much Jesus talked about judgment (Matthew 13:36-43,47-50;

Is the God of the Old Testament
the Same God of the New Testament?

121

25:41-46; Luke 12:4-5; 16:19-31). It's stunning. And to top this all off, simply read the book of Revelation and you can quickly see that God is a just God (Revelation 20:11-15).

Upon closer inspection, it is clear that the Bible does not portray a dual-headed, bipolar god who suffers from an identity crisis, nor does the New Testament create a theological wedge between two separate gods. Rather the entire Bible unveils for us one multifaceted God who is both just *and* gracious.

■ Thought to Ponder
The justice of God and the grace of God are not at odds.

■ Memory Verse
> The LORD waits to be gracious to you,
>> and therefore he exalts himself to show mercy to you.
> For the LORD is a God of justice;
>> blessed are all those who wait for him.
>
> (Isaiah 30:18)

■ Question to Consider
Can you think of any other examples of God's grace in the Old Testament and His justice in the New Testament?

■ One-Minute Apologist Video
Bobby Conway, "Is the God of the NT and OT the Same?"
www.youtube.com/watch?v=wIVHZHih1As

Will Heaven Be Boring?

If you are not allowed to laugh in heaven, I don't want to go there.

Martin Luther

We've all heard the descriptions of heaven being a place where we will float on clouds, play a harp, and inherit our own set of wings. Fortunately, all three of those descriptions are dead wrong. First, we won't float on clouds. Second, everyone won't play a harp. And third, no believer will inherit a set of wings. Wings are for angels, and the last time I checked, humans aren't angels. It's cheesy descriptions like this that make heaven seem so dreadful and unappealing. Throw in the idea of heaven lasting forever, and our minds can really start to reel. We may think, *At some point heaven will surely become boring.*

Just the other night my wife, Heather, confessed her struggle to understand heaven. She expressed the difficulty she has with the idea of forever. It's hard for her to imagine an environment being so wonderful and so perfect that she'd want to live there forever and ever and ever and ever and ever. The very idea of forever messes with her head, and heaven will be a forever place. While I won't pretend to know a lot about heaven (because I don't, nor do I think anyone does), I will say that heaven will be far from boring.

Heaven will be like the party you never wanted to leave, and guess what—you won't have to. And better yet, you won't *want* to leave. Thinking of heaven that way helps me to understand how I could exist in a forever place without growing weary. Besides, who wouldn't want to exist forever in a place with God, angels, redeemed family, friends, and fellow believers all accompanied with perfect health, joy, and peace, with no guilt or sin, not even sadness, but just an eternal state of completion and ultimate satisfaction?

That description barely scratches the surface, but it's enough for me to see that with that kind of fulfillment, heaven will be far from boring. And Heather agrees.

■ Thought to Ponder

Here's a guarantee: if being a Christian on earth isn't boring, then certainly being a Christian in heaven won't be boring.

■ Memory Verse

What no eye has seen, nor ear heard, nor the heart of man imagined, what God has prepared for those who love him— these things God has revealed to us through the Spirit. For the Spirit searches everything, even the depths of God (1 Corinthians 2:9-10).

■ Question to Consider

If heaven is supposed to be so great, why do you think so many Christians seemingly lack excitement about going there?

■ One-Minute Apologist Video

Bobby Conway, "Will Heaven Be Boring?"
www.youtube.com/watch?v=MilOotKtyTg

What Is Hell in a Nutshell?

> *Scripture sees hell as self-chosen...Hell appears*
> *as God's gesture of respect for human choice.*
> *All receive what they actually chose, either*
> *to be with God forever, worshipping him, or*
> *without God forever, worshipping themselves.*
>
> J.I. PACKER

No other doctrine in all of Scripture has troubled me more than the doctrine of hell. The thought of people eternally existing apart from God is heartbreaking—as I suppose it should be. As much as I like the idea that all people will ultimately be saved, I just don't see the biblical evidence for that view.

The teaching of hell in Scripture crystallizes through progressive revelation. In the Old Testament the word *Sheol* was used to describe the invisible place of the dead, for both believers and nonbelievers alike. The New Testament equivalent to Sheol is the Greek word *Hades*. It too is a place of the unseen. Second Peter 2:4 uses the word *Tartarus* to describe a deep place beneath the earth where God pours out His judgment.

However, the most popular word used in the Bible to describe hell was *Gehenna*. Translated into Greek, the Hebrew "Valley of Hinnom" becomes *Gehenna* (Matthew 5:22; Mark 9:43,45,47; Luke 12:5; James 3:6). This was a place where parents once sacrificed their children as a burnt offering to Molech (2 Kings 23:10;

2 Chronicles 28:3; 33:6). The Valley of Hinnom was also used as a garbage dump where waste burned continually. This became the graphic description Jesus used for hell, not to describe a literal fire, but to explain in metaphorical terms the horrific reality of being separated from God. The metaphorical use of words is not uncommon in the Bible. For example, James describes the tongue as a fire too (James 3:6). He used the term to describe how destructive the tongue could be, not to say that the tongue is a *literal* fire. In the same way, Jesus describes hell metaphorically to demonstrate its harsh reality.

As we read our Bibles, here is what we discover about hell. It was prepared for Satan and his demons (Matthew 25:41). Hell is eternal (Matthew 25:46; Revelation 20:10). It's a place of conscious torment (2 Thessalonians 1:5-10; Revelation 14:9-11). It's the destiny of all nonbelievers (Revelation 20:15). And there is a gradation of punishment in hell, which corresponds to one's iniquities (Matthew 11:20-24).

With this biblical understanding, hell can be defined as follows: *hell is an eternal place of conscious torment whereby God's justifiable wrath is poured out on Satan, his demons, and unrepentant sinners.* In light of this awful reality, the most unloving thing we can do is remain silent about hell. We owe it to our fellow humans to lovingly implore them to place their faith in Jesus Christ.

▪ Thought to Ponder

No other doctrine is harder to square with God's unconditional love than the doctrine of hell.

▪ Memory Verse

If anyone's name was not found written in the book of life, he was thrown into the lake of fire (Revelation 20:15).

■ Question to Consider
How can hell be squared with God's unconditional love?

■ One-Minute Apologist Video
Bobby Conway, "What Is Hell in a Nutshell?"
www.youtube.com/watch?v=FIot0DtBXCs

Is Purgatory Biblical?

> *Purgatory is a vital component in a spirituality of works-righteousness that rests upon the attaining of merit rather than justification by free grace.*
>
> DONALD BLOESCH

Purgatory is a Roman Catholic teaching primarily discovered in the apocryphal book of 2 Maccabees 12:43-46. Essentially, purgatory is a place where those who died in "God's grace" go to be "purged" of their pardonable sins before going to be with God in heaven. As attractive as this idea may be to some, purgatory is not without problems.

First, this teaching is rooted in the Apocrypha. This is important to note as the Apocrypha wasn't accepted as part of the biblical canon by Jews and Protestants. As Christians our teaching about the afterlife is derived first and foremost from those books that are fully accepted as Scripture.

Second, purgatory fails to recognize the total sufficiency of the cross. It does so by having those who died in grace pay the penalty dished out to them for their venial (forgivable) sins. Instead of the cross being sufficient, the person in purgatory adds a bit to Christ's finished work in order to make their way to heaven.

Third, Jesus and His disciples never teach about purgatory. This is crucial. If purgatory were indeed part of God's plan of salvation, you would think there'd be New Testament evidence for it.

But there's not. Purgatory is without a trace in the New Testament. And any argument used to justify it from the New Testament is found wanting.

Fourth, purgatory directly contradicts Scripture. Hebrews 9:27 says, "It is appointed for man to die once, and after that comes judgment." Where did the thief on the cross go when he died? Jesus said to him, "Truly, I say to you, today you will be with me in Paradise" (Luke 23:43). He didn't say, "You'll first be purged." If anyone could use a little purging, it was the thief on the cross, yet he was ushered directly into Paradise.

Regrettably, purgatory leaves many people believing they'll spend a period of time being purged for their smaller sins. Thankfully, we are declared righteous by God's grace, and it's His mercy that suits us for heaven, not a post-mortem season of purging. Big or small, *all* sins are cleared at the cross for believers. Jesus said it best, "It is finished" (John 19:30).

▪ Thought to Ponder

If purgatory is true, then the atonement didn't pay for all of our sins.

▪ Memory Verse

It is appointed for man to die once, and after that comes judgment (Hebrews 9:27).

▪ Question to Consider

Why is purgatory an attractive doctrine to some people?

▪ One-Minute Apologist Video

Bobby Conway, "Is Purgatory Biblical?"
www.youtube.com/watch?v=ndPWE4oNhbc

What Are the Marks of a Cult?

> *The philosophical method of the central figures in cults is to take a partial truth—such as a verse used as a proof-text—and blend it with an untruth so that the mix has the appearance of interpretation but in reality is systematically false.*
>
> RAVI ZACHARIAS

In today's religiously eclectic culture, labeling a group a cult may step on a few toes, but never have ideas moved about so abundantly as they do today. We live in a sound-bite culture where information is multiplying at rapid speeds, and there's no shortage of false truth claims hanging out in this world filled with so many clashing ideas.

Dealing with false teaching is nothing new. John the apostle writes, "Beloved, do not believe every spirit, but test the spirits to see whether they are from God, for many false prophets have gone out into the world" (1 John 4:1). If the early church needed to exercise discernment, how much more so do we two thousand years later? Here are two simple marks to discern as it relates to cults.

A cult can be marked theologically. This is seen in their rejection of one or more of the core Christian doctrines *or* by their addition to those doctrines. Typically, a cult is marked by added revelation,

a distorted view of Christ, a dismissal of original sin, a deconstruct-
ing of the Trinity, a redefining of grace, and a works-based salvation.

A cult can be marked sociologically. Cults are often brainwashed
by an ultra-authoritarian leader, as in the tragic case of David
Koresh, the Branch Davidian leader in Waco, Texas. Or an ultra-
authoritarian organization, such as the Watch Tower Society that
oversees the cultic group known as Jehovah's Witnesses. These
leaders and organizations create a sociological wedge between
their followers and the world, which inevitably promotes iso-
lationism. Cult leaders often dictate what their followers are to
believe, think, speak, feel, eat, drink, and even wear. Some cults
are easy to identify, while others are more difficult for the less discerning to detect.

In order to recognize a cult, you must first be theologically
rooted in your own faith. Be sure to be a student of Scripture.
Once you are biblically grounded, compare what Mormons or
Jehovah's Witnesses say about Jesus, the Trinity, salvation, the cross,
eternity, Scripture, and sin. You'll find that they may use some of
the same lingo, but their beliefs, when contrasted with Christianity, are worlds apart.

■ Thought to Ponder

Next time a Mormon or a Jehovah's Witness knocks at your door,
view it as God's open door to share the true Christ with them.

■ Memory Verse

Beloved, do not believe every spirit, but test the spirits to see
whether they are from God (1 John 4:1).

Question to Consider

The word *cult* isn't a popular word these days. When you think of a cult, what comes to your mind?

One-Minute Apologist Video

Richard Howe, "What Is a Cult?"
www.youtube.com/watch?v=nvvSuvSA3EI

Should Christians Burn the Koran?

Though we cannot think alike
may we not love alike?

John Wesley

Terry Jones is a Florida pastor who a few years ago promoted the idea of burning copies of the Koran. This infamous Koran-burning fanatic hasn't helped the church in the reputation department before the broader world. I'm thankful that most people are wise enough to know that Jones doesn't represent the heartbeat of most Christians. While we as Christians do reject the teachings of the Koran, that doesn't grant us the right to burn the Muslim's holy book. There's no quicker way to burn a relational bridge with the Muslim community than to burn the Koran.

Now, there is a story in the book of Acts about some recent converts to Christianity who burned their sorcery books. In Acts 19:19 we read, "And a number of those who had practiced magic arts brought their books together and burned them in the sight of all. And they counted the value of them and found it came to fifty thousand pieces of silver." Some might contend, "See, we have a proof text for burning the Koran." But the people involved in the book burning in the book of Acts were those who actually *practiced* sorcery and magic. They burned their own books as a symbol of their repentance from magic to the Messiah. It was a sign that they were abandoning a life of sorcery to follow hard after Jesus. It wasn't a propaganda stunt. It would be more like a Muslim becoming a Christian and burning his own Koran. While I wouldn't encourage that, it is still a lot different from a Christian burning a Koran in his angry frustration against Islam.

In the end, we need to ask ourselves, "Why in the world would we want to offend the very people we are trying to reach with the gospel?" Christ called us to build bridges, not burn them.

■ Thought to Ponder

Muslims, like all people, deserve our greatest respect as people created in the image of God. They aren't our enemies; they're humans in desperate need of the gospel.

■ Memory Verse

As you wish that others would do to you, do so to them (Luke 6:31).

■ Question to Consider

Instead of burning the Koran, what are some ways Christians can build relational bridges with Muslims?

■ One-Minute Apologist Video

Bobby Conway, "Should Christians Burn the Quran?" www.youtube.com/watch?v=ChHSnS64my8

QUESTION 46

Do All Religions
Lead to Heaven?

Let us consider, that, in matters of religion,
whatever is different is contrary; and that it
is impossible the religions of ancient Rome,
of Turkey, of Siam, and of China, all of them,
be established on any sound foundation.

DAVID HUME

Perhaps you've heard the statement, "Getting to heaven is like climbing a mountain. Both have many paths, but they all lead to the top." While that may be true for climbing a mountain, it's not true for getting to heaven. Heaven's architect, Jesus Christ, clearly stated, "I am the way, and the truth, and the life. No one comes to the Father except through me" (John 14:6). Jesus's claim runs counter to the pluralistic contention that all roads lead to heaven. He said, "I am the way to heaven." If there were another way to heaven, Jesus would've been a fool to die on the cross. The cross shouts out, "Pluralism is false."

If you read Scripture, you will quickly see that God's never been a pluralist. He's never said, "Just pick a god and head my direction." In the Old Testament the Israelites got themselves into trouble when they started collecting the gods of the nations surrounding them. As a result, they were sent into captivity. That's because

God's not a fan of pluralism. He knows that no other gods exist—that He alone is God.

The belief that pluralism is true crumbles once you juxtapose the other faiths against Christianity. Hindus and Buddhists believe in samsara, a continuous cycle of life, death, and reincarnation whereby they hope to one day be set free. Muslims believe that Allah will weigh our works, and if our righteous acts outweigh our unrighteous acts, we may have a shot at getting into heaven. Atheists believe that death is the end. It's lights out and there is no heaven.

So, which is it—samsara, scales, or no heaven in the first place? This mere sampling reveals the contradictions. Not all of these beliefs can be true. They may all be wrong, but they can't all be true. When Jesus was asked about truth, He claimed, "I am...the truth." On the cross Jesus became heaven's visible GPS. It turns out that He's our true north after all. He is the *only* way to heaven.

Now, this may produce a secondary question for you. If religious pluralism is false and Jesus is the only way to heaven, then what's the fate of those who've never heard about Jesus? This is one of the most difficult, if not the most difficult, questions for me personally. And there's no easy *emotional* answer. Nevertheless, no worldview comes without its hard questions. This happens to be one of our hard questions as Christians. And I think we need to admit it. It's hard. Nevertheless, here are some principles that I've tried to remember when I find myself struggling to cope with the fate of those who've never heard:

- God passionately loves the world (John 3:16).

- God's not willing that any should perish (2 Peter 3:9).

- God's nature is just and He will do what is right (Genesis 18:25).

- God takes no pleasure in the death of the wicked (Ezekiel 18:23).

- God went to great lengths to save us (Romans 5:8).

- God has provided both general and special revelation (Romans 1:20; 2:14-15).

- None of us will have an excuse (Romans 1:20).

While these principles don't eliminate my angst in full, they at least cultivate a biblical view of God's character and remind me that I can trust Him to do what is right.

■ Thought to Ponder
Just because there are many paths to the top of a mountain doesn't mean there are many paths to God.

■ Memory Verse
There is salvation in no one else, for there is no other name under heaven given among men by which we must be saved (Acts 4:12).

■ Question to Consider
If there are other ways to heaven, then why did Jesus die so we could get there?

■ One-Minute Apologist Video
Erwin Lutzer, "Why Is Jesus the Only One Qualified?"
www.youtube.com/watch?v=eCDGDXqQNI0

Is Baptism Necessary for Salvation?

> *Baptism is the discarded jewel of Christian churches today.*
>
> MARK DEVER

There is a lot of confusion about baptism today, and many end up at one of two extremes. At one end are people who exclaim, "Baptism is necessary for salvation." At the other end are people who avoid baptism altogether. What do we do with this tension? For starters, realize that both extremes are *extreme*.

Baptism is *not* necessary for salvation. If it were, Paul the apostle never would have said, "For Christ did not send me to baptize but to preach the gospel" (1 Corinthians 1:17a). Paul valued baptism dearly, but preaching the gospel was his core concern because he knew that receiving the gospel by faith was the necessary ingredient for salvation.

However, Jesus did expect believers to be baptized. He commissioned His disciples, saying, "Go therefore and make disciples of all nations, baptizing them in the name of the Father and of the Son and of the Holy Spirit" (Matthew 28:19).

But beyond the fact that baptism is commanded, it also provides a wonderful opportunity to demonstrate our faith in Jesus Christ publicly, to depict outwardly what took place inwardly. Going under the water of baptism shows that you identify with

Christ's death and burial, and coming out of the water demonstrates that you identify with His resurrection, which enables you to walk in newness of life.

Furthermore, in the early church, baptism was taken very seriously. It was seen as a necessary part of Christian discipleship, as it should be today. However, here's something to consider. If baptism were necessary for salvation, the thief on the cross would've never been saved. That's worth pondering. Therefore, as important as it is, baptism was never meant to be a salvation issue; it is a discipleship issue. Note the difference.

▨ Thought to Ponder

Baptism isn't commanded for salvation; it's commanded to commemorate it.

▨ Memory Verse

Baptism, which corresponds to this, now saves you, not as a removal of dirt from the body but as an appeal to God for a good conscience, through the resurrection of Jesus Christ (1 Peter 3:21).

▨ Question to Consider

How can the church do a better job of stressing the correct view of baptism before the church and challenging unbaptized believers to get baptized?

▨ One-Minute Apologist Video

Bobby Conway, "Is Baptism Necessary for Salvation?" www.youtube.com/watch?v=75UDydZly6k

What Is Apologetics?

Apologetics is to be seen not as a defensive and hostile reaction against the world, but as a welcome opportunity to exhibit, celebrate, and display the treasure chest of the Christian faith.

ALISTAIR MCGRATH

Like most people, the first time I heard the word *apologetics* I was befuddled. I was driving down Interstate 5 in Southern California en route to work at the Ritz-Carlton Hotel, and for the life of me I couldn't understand why there was such a stress for Christians to apologize. After showing up at work, I asked a fellow Christian what the word meant, and that's when I discovered, to my relief, that *apologetics* means to defend the faith.

The word comes from the Greek *apologia*, meaning "to defend." We see this word used in 1 Peter 3:15 where Peter says, "always being prepared to make a defense (*apologia*) to anyone who asks you for a reason for the hope that is in you; yet do it with gentleness and respect." Let's unpack this verse and glean a few insights from it.

First, Peter says, "Always being prepared to make a defense." In order to make a defense, we must be prepared—or at least be preparing. We need to love the world enough to care about their questions. We can start by tackling the most common objections nonbelievers have to the Christian faith, many of which are discussed briefly in this book.

Second, Peter tells us "to make a defense to anyone who asks you for a reason for the hope that is in you." This inner hope relates to our faith in Jesus Christ. Be ready to talk about the difference Jesus has made in your life. God wants to use our hope to instill hope in others.

Third, Peter tells us to defend our faith with "gentleness and respect." Regrettably, apologetics has been given a bad rap at times since some apologists come off as arrogant. That's really unfortunate. And it's exactly what Peter warns against. He tells us to defend the truth gently *and* respectfully. Tone matters when communicating truth. Gentleness and respect also go a long way in creating relational harmony.

What you say and how you say it are both crucial. It's not either/or. It's truth and love.

The need for apologetics has never been greater. In our pluralistic and secularized culture, we need a batch of Christians who are not only aware of their beliefs, but also get the gist of the beliefs of those around them. This melting pot of beliefs has caused many to question truth altogether. The confusion is systemic, and apologetics can be a great tool for providing some much needed clarity. So prepare well. And "contend for the faith that was once for all delivered to the saints" (Jude 3).

▣ Thought to Ponder
Apologetics provides credible answers to compelling questions.

▣ Memory Verse
In your hearts honor Christ the Lord as holy, always being prepared to make a defense to anyone who asks you for a reason for the hope that is in you; yet do it with gentleness and respect (1 Peter 3:15).

■ Question to Consider

What are the greatest objections that nonbelievers have against Christianity?

■ One-Minute Apologist Video

Frank Turek, "What Is Apologetics?"
www.youtube.com/watch?v=fDo31cccnTo

What Is the Heart of Apologetics?

> *The gospel which we possess was not given to us only to be admired, talked of, and professed, but to be practiced.*
>
> J.C. RYLE

When people think about apologetics they usually don't associate the word with "heart." That's because apologetics has been unfortunately relegated to just the head. But apologetics should involve both head *and* heart. During the Last Supper with His disciples, Jesus said, "A new commandment I give to you, that you love one another: just as I have loved you, you also are to love one another. By this all people will know that you are my disciples, if you have love for one another" (John 13:34-35).

When we think about apologetics, we often think about giving heady arguments to defend the reliability of Christianity. We carefully lay out our arguments for the existence of God, the infallibility of Scripture, the empty tomb, and so on. Yet here Jesus says, "I've got a 'hearty' apologetic for you." Jesus says if you want to give a great defense of Christianity, then do so by loving each other "just as I have loved you."

Now that's a tall order, isn't it? Expounding on Jesus's words, the late apologist Francis Schaeffer said,

Yet, without true Christians loving one another, Christ says the world cannot be expected to listen, even when we give proper answers. Let us be careful, indeed, to spend a lifetime studying to give honest answers. For years the orthodox, evangelical church has done this very poorly. So it is well to spend time learning to answer the questions of men who are about us. But after we have done our best to communicate to a lost world, still we must never forget that the final apologetic which Jesus gives is the observable love of true Christians for true Christians.*

As Christians, we are to be salt and light (Matthew 5:13-14). It's hard to impact our culture if we turn people off by the way we live. Our life is meant to be an apologetic. Without love, our apologetic is powerless. We are like a noisy gong (1 Corinthians 13:1). The heartbeat of apologetics is spelled with four letters: L-O-V-E. It turns out that love is far easier to spell out than it is to live out.

▪ Thought to Ponder

The gospel is meant to be more than defended. It must be displayed.

▪ Memory Verse

By this all people will know that you are my disciples, if you have love for one another (John 13:35).

▪ Question to Consider

Do you think apologetics focuses enough on the importance of displaying our faith as a form of defense before the watching world?

---

* Francis Schaeffer, *The Great Evangelical Disaster* (Westchester, IL: Crossway Books, 1984), 164-65.

■ One-Minute Apologist Video

Eric Metaxas, "When Is Logic Not Enough?"
www.youtube.com/watch?v=mI0gwIUIJMA

Resurrection: Fact or Fiction?

If Jesus rose from the dead, then you have to accept all that he said; if he didn't rise from the dead, then why worry about any of what he said? The issue on which everything hangs is not whether or not you like his teaching but whether or not he rose from the dead.

TIMOTHY KELLER

Following the first Easter Sunday, it didn't take long for people to come up with fictitious claims to debunk the resurrection of Jesus Christ. They knew that if they could cast doubt on the resurrection, Christianity would crumble. In fact, Paul writes, "If Christ has not been raised, your faith is futile and you are still in your sins" (1 Corinthians 15:17).

Here are a few theories that critics of the resurrection sought to advance:

Jesus's body was stolen. This was the first theory proposed. But if Jesus's body had really been stolen, don't you think the thieves would have produced the body once the disciples claimed "He has risen"? They would have called the disciples' bluff. Guaranteed. And if the disciples stole the body—the story the Jewish leaders came up with (Matthew 28:11-15)—do you think they would have died martyrs' deaths for a hoax? Of course not. As it's been said before, "Many will die for what they think to be true, but no one will die for what they know to be false."

The people were hallucinating. Scoffers said that the witnesses who claimed to have seen Jesus after His death must have been hallucinating. However, Jesus appeared to a number of people on several different occasions following His resurrection, and on one occasion, He appeared to more than five hundred people at once (1 Corinthians 15:3-8). Now in my pre-Jesus party days, I understood hallucination, and I can tell you that five hundred people don't hallucinate like that. They saw something. They saw Him. Alive.

Jesus passed out. This is known as the "swoon theory." Popularized in the eighteenth century, it suggests that Jesus didn't actually die on the cross but merely passed out. Then once inside the tomb, He regained consciousness and rolled the stone away Himself. But ponder this. Jesus had been so severely scourged that He had to have the help of Simon of Cyrene to carry His cross (see Luke 23:26). His head had multiple puncture wounds from the crown of thorns, His wrists and ankles had been nailed to the cross, and He had been stabbed in the side. After He was taken down from the cross, His body was wrapped in seventy-five pounds of linen. Do you think Jesus could have regained consciousness, unwrapped Himself, and moved a two-ton stone out of the way?

The fact is...Jesus is alive. Sometimes it's just easier to believe the facts than create fiction. So go ahead; stick your head in the tomb. You see, it's empty and the *living* Jesus is ready to change your life. Today.

■ **Thought to Ponder**

The tomb became empty so our lives could become full.

■ Memory Verse

He is not here, for he has risen, as he said. Come, see the place where he lay (Matthew 28:6).

■ Question to Consider

Why do you think some nonbelievers are so quick to dismiss the resurrection of Jesus Christ?

■ One-Minute Apologist Video

Gary Habermas, "The Resurrection,"
www.youtube.com/watch?v=v2y8S2ACBRA

Is There Evidence for the Resurrection?

> *Resurrection means that the worst thing is never the last thing.*
>
> FREDERICK BUECHNER

I have struggled with doubt for years. I'm part of the Thomas Tribe. I don't like it, but my mind just works that way. And at times, it's been horrifying, lonely, and even deeply depressing. I'm an obsessive analyzer. I don't know how to turn my mind off. I fixate and sometimes sink into the quicksand of doubt.

But here's what else I can tell you. When I struggle with doubt, I go back to the resurrection. And here's why—I can't get around the evidence. I've tried. Not because I want to get around the evidence but to see if I can, to test the strength of the resurrection.

I'm thankful that the resurrection of Jesus Christ comes fully furnished with solid evidence. It's critical that it does, because our faith hangs on this crucial event in history. Remember the apostle Paul's shocking statement that I cited in the previous chapter? "And if Christ has not been raised, your faith is futile and you are still in your sins" (1 Corinthians 15:17). That's jaw dropping. Paul is basically saying, "Hey Christians, our faith rises and falls on the resurrection."

I hate to say it, but if Jesus didn't rise from the dead, we are deceived Christians. We've been duped. We've bought a lie and we're anesthetizing ourselves on a mere fairytale. So if our faith isn't fiction, what evidence is there for the resurrection? In short, here are five lines of evidence.

First, women were the first to discover the empty tomb. Why is this critical? It is well known and unfortunate that the testimony of women in the ancient world wasn't highly regarded. If the authors of the Gospels were making up this story, they wouldn't have fabricated women as the first witnesses of the resurrection. Rather, they would've had bona fide witnesses as the first discoverers of the empty tomb.

Second, the empty tomb is evidence for the resurrection. Even after the disciples were claiming that Jesus rose from the dead, no one was able to call their bluff. And that's because they weren't bluffing. As we discussed in the previous chapter, if the disciples stole the body of Jesus, do you think they would have died for a lie? And if some nonbelievers stole Jesus's body, they most assuredly would've brought it out into the open once the rumor began spreading that Jesus rose from the dead.

Third, post-resurrection appearances provide further evidence for Jesus's resurrection. As I said in the previous chapter, Jesus appeared to His followers on several different occasions, and He even appeared to more than five hundred at one time. By doing so, Jesus was establishing visible evidence for His eyewitnesses that He had defeated the grave.

Fourth, fulfilled prophecy served as another line of evidence for Jesus's resurrection. His resurrection was prophesied in the Old Testament (Psalm 16:9-10) and Jesus Himself prophesied His own resurrection in the New Testament (Matthew 12:40; Mark 14:58; John 2:18-22).

Finally, you can't explain the early church and the radical life change of Jesus's disciples apart from the resurrection. The disciples saw something. These once fearful disciples, who could hardly follow Jesus during His earthly ministry, would now willingly lay down their lives for Him. That's because they saw a living Jesus and experienced a radical life change. His resurrection turned doubting Thomas into a great missionary, denying Peter into a bold preacher, and adversary Paul into a tireless advocate of the gospel.

The case for the resurrection is so robust that many skeptics through the ages have become sincere followers of Jesus Christ in light of all the evidence. Now that's exciting.

■ Thought to Ponder

The resurrection of Jesus Christ is the exclamation point to the truthfulness of Christianity.

■ Memory Verse

If Christ has not been raised, then our preaching is in vain and your faith is in vain (1 Corinthians 15:14).

■ Question to Consider

Can you think of any other evidence to demonstrate a case for the resurrection?

■ One-Minute Apologist Video

Bobby Conway, "Proofs of the Resurrection of Jesus Christ?" www.youtube.com/watch?v=RzNREgNC11k

How Do I Deal With My Doubts?

There is enough light for those who want to believe and enough shadows to blind those who don't.

BLAISE PASCAL

H ave you ever doubted your faith? If so, you aren't alone. Doubt isn't an exclusively Christian problem. It's a human problem. To be human is to be susceptible to doubt.

Atheists doubt.

Pluralists doubt.

Buddhists doubt.

Hindus doubt.

Muslims doubt.

And yes, Christians doubt too.

Ours is a world of uncertainty, and that can create a bit of a fit for some of us who belong to the doubters' club. Doubt is no respecter of beliefs; we're all vulnerable. That's because we're *human*.

Human doubt harkens back to the Garden of Eden, where the serpent deceptively posed the question, "Did God actually say...?" (Genesis 3:1). And this question has been posed billions of times ever since. Doubt is replete in Scripture. Be it Job, Sarah, Abraham, Habakkuk, David, Gideon, Zechariah, Thomas, Peter, or even John the Baptist, doubt has a way of catching up with all of us at some point during our earthly sojourn.

Here are four shades of doubt that people often bump up against.

First, there's emotional doubt. This is the doubt you feel when you experience or observe evil or unbearable suffering in the world, and you find yourself thinking, "How can a good God allow this to happen?" Emotional doubt is what you feel when you doubt the security of your own salvation. Or the angst of losing a loved one or finding out that you've got a terminal disease. It's taxing, and God often feels totally absent during this season.

Second, there's intellectual doubt. This is where you find yourself doubting the validity of the Christian faith. You catch yourself asking, "Can I trust the Bible? Are miracles possible? Did Jesus really die for me?" Intellectual doubt was what Thomas experienced when he doubted Christ's resurrection. This type of doubt can make you feel like you're losing your mind as you throw your hands up in despair.

Third, there's volitional doubt. This is a battle of the wills. There's God's way and our way, and unfortunately these two often clash. We wonder, "Does God really know what's best for my life?" We think, "Should I really lay down my desires and trust God to lead me?" The volitional doubter is in a spiritual tug-of-war with God, but must yield to discover true blessing. Jesus beautifully modeled the surrendered life when He prayed, "Nevertheless, not my will, but yours, be done" (Luke 22:42).

Fourth, there's moral doubt. This shade of doubt is frequently caused by sin or even questioning whether God's moral standards are legit or up-to-date enough. It may be related to premarital sex or homosexuality or smoking dope or cross-dressing or pornography. You name it. Moral doubt grips us when we're tempted to relativize God's moral truth. As a result, people frequently cave in to sin, and God's moral standards are ignored. Sin has a heart-hardening component to it that can spiritually blind us to truth. It has a way of deceiving us. So be on guard and take hold of the lost art of confession by keeping short accounts with God.

In my book *Doubting Toward Faith,* I deal more in-depth with these shades or facets of doubt. (I also discuss there what I call evidential doubt.) Given these varieties of doubt, how can we deal with our doubts?

Here's some quick advice:

- Recognize your shade(s) of doubt.

- Identify what's triggering your doubts.

- Find some trusted friends who will help you process your doubts out loud.

- Write your particular doubts down and rank the ones that trouble you the most.

- Begin chasing down the answers to the questions that most disturb you.

- Relentlessly seek after God's heart.

- Discover your doubt patterns through consistent journaling.

- Realize that *no* belief system can completely close the doubt gap, so don't demand certainty, lest you set yourself up for disillusionment.

- And remember that God can use your doubts to strengthen you and help others.

That should get you started.

So get after it.

■ **Thought to Ponder**

Doubt is not the opposite of faith. Unbelief is.

■ **Memory Verse**

Have mercy on those who doubt (Jude 22).

■ **Question to Consider**

Why do you think there's such a rise of doubt in today's culture?

■ **One-Minute Apologist Video**

Os Guinness, "How Can a Christian Deal with Doubt?"
www.youtube.com/watch?v=gY0DXkXhUE4

About the Author

Bobby Conway is lead pastor of Life Fellowship Church near Charlotte, North Carolina. He is a graduate of Dallas Theological Seminary (ThM), Southern Evangelical Seminary (DMin), and is a PhD candidate in philosophy of religion at the University of Birmingham in England. Bobby is the author of *Hell, Rob Bell and What Happens When People Die*, *The Fifth Gospel*, and *Doubting Toward Faith*, and he's also the founder and host of the One Minute Apologist (http://oneminuteapol ogist.com). Bobby and his wife live in North Carolina with their two teenagers, Haley and Dawson.

To learn more about Harvest House books and
to read sample chapters, visit our website:

www.harvesthousepublishers.com

HARVEST HOUSE PUBLISHERS
EUGENE, OREGON